More Than a Job!

Helping Your Teenagers Find Success and Satisfaction in Their Future Careers

• Richard T. Lapan •

AMERICAN COUNSELING ASSOCIATION
5999 Stevenson Avenue
Alexandria, VA 22304
www.counseling.org

More Than a Job!

Helping Your Teenagers Find Success and Satisfaction in Their Future Careers

10 9 8 7 6 5 4 3 2 1

American Counseling Association
5999 Stevenson Avenue • Alexandria, VA 22304

Director of Publications • Carolyn C. Baker

Production Manager • Bonny E. Gaston

Copy Editor • Kay Mikel

Editorial Assistant • Catherine A. Brumley

Cover illustration by Kaylin Lapan.

Text design by Bonny E. Gaston.

Library of Congress Cataloging-in-Publication Data
Lapan, Richard T.
More than a job! : helping your teenagers find success and satisfaction in their future careers / Richard T. Lapan.
p. cm.
Includes bibliographical references.
ISBN 978-1-55620-278-0 (alk. paper)
1. Teenagers—Vocational guidance. 2. Vocational guidance. I. Title.
HF5381.L316 2007
650.10835—dc22 2007025962

• Dedication •

To my loving wife and lifelong partner
Sharon Loehr Lapan

• Contents •

• About the Author •

Dr. Lapan is a professor and chair of the Department of Student Development and Pupil Personnel Services at the University of Massachusetts Amherst. He is a counselor educator and a psychologist committed to transforming the profession of school counseling from an ancillary support service to a comprehensive program central to the academic and social missions of every school. The effectiveness of these efforts was recognized in 2006 when Dr. Lapan won the prestigious Counselor Educator of the Year award from the American School Counselor Association. In 1972, Dr. Lapan received his BA from St. Anselm's College (majoring in philosophy). He earned his master's degree in 1974 from Duquesne University (in existential/phenomenological counseling). In 1986, Dr. Lapan graduated with distinction from the University of Utah, receiving a PhD in counseling psychology.

Dr. Lapan has had extensive experience providing counseling services (career, family, individual, group, and residential) to children, adolescents, and adults. From 1975 until 1980, he worked as a master's-level counselor providing counseling, educational, and residential treatment services for urban, suburban, and rural adolescents. He has worked in several school settings and psychiatric hospitals. After completing his doctorate, Dr. Lapan provided career counseling services to adults who were in the process of making significant career and life changes.

In 2004, Dr. Lapan published *Career Development Across the K–16 Years: Bridging the Present to Satisfying and Successful Futures.* This book synthesizes the research in this field and outlines the integrative contextual model of career development. This resource served as an important foundation for the approach and practices recommended in this current book for parents. Dr. Lapan has published numerous empirical studies on a wide range of career development topics (from the process of compromise adolescents engage in when orienting themselves toward the world of work to the entry of women into nontraditional science-related careers). In 2000, Dr. Lapan received the Distinguished Service Award from the Guidance Division of the Association for Career and Technical Education. His work has consistently emphasized expanding meaningful and satisfying career opportunities for all of our young people.

• Acknowledgments •

For more than 25 years, my wife, Sharon, has used her creativity, problem-solving skills, and art talents to help a diverse range of K–12 students fall in love with learning. She has been a source of support and hope for many parents struggling to help their children. In our relationship, I have certainly gained more than I have given. She successfully empowered each of our three daughters to create their own personal and career identities. Many of the ideas presented in this book are better because of Sharon's insights and contributions. The older I get the more I realize that no one does anything of import by themselves. By reading and using this book, you too will benefit from Sharon's skills and insights into how we can help adolescents create meaningful, purposeful, and satisfying ways to live in this world.

To write this book, I have drawn from my now 22 years of experience as a Dad. I couldn't be prouder of my three daughters or love them more. Each treats others well, tries her hardest, and is not afraid to take risks that lead to self-determination and identity development. I have learned much from being their parent and hope that this book captures some of this for other parents.

I have been very fortunate to learn from and work with terrific colleagues. In particular, the following friends have been of enormous help in the development of this book: Dr. Norman Gysbers, University of Missouri-Columbia; Drs. Jay Carey, Carey Dimmit, and Mary Lynn Boscardin, University of Massachusetts Amherst; Karen DeCoster, Massachusetts Department of Education; Dr. David Blustein, Boston College; and Sarah Holden, an enormously talented student soon to graduate from our school counseling master's program at the University of Massachusetts Amherst. I thank each of you for your help, friendship, and support.

• First, The Big Picture •

It's kind of a Catch-22, because at the time you're finishing high school, you have no idea what you want to do with your life. Yet you're making the most important decisions about where it's going.

—Fifth year Michigan State University senior, *USA Today*

• Hope •

My middle daughter left home for college this fall. Such an easy sentence to write for an event that has upended my family's emotional life and laid claim to lots of our money for many years to come. Fortunately, 3 months in she has found her bearings and is both happy and productive.

Beginning around 11th grade, my wife and I noticed a different kind of self-understanding starting to take root inside of our daughter. This became evident in the choices she made about the classes she took, friends she hung out with, and the after school and summer activities she joined in on. Soon thereafter she began to identify college options that would get her closer to these dreams. When I asked her what it was about this direction that was so appealing, she said with great joy: "It's everything that I like to do all linked together." This focus required my daughter to fit together and exploit a wide range of her talents, interests, and values. It connected her present to a future she really wants to live. It helped her to experience a new level of satisfaction, purpose, and meaning in her high school coursework and in life outside of school.

• Career Identity •

One of the most important developmental challenges your children will face is the creation of a career identity that will help them act in the present and move toward the future with a sense of hopefulness, purpose, and direction. Ideally, your teenagers' decision to pursue a career path will be an expression of a direction in life that means something very important to them. It is an enormous opportunity for creative self-definition, a chance to imbue what they do to make a living with meaning and purpose. Satisfaction with one's work and satisfaction with one's life are highly intertwined. A career path that enables your teenagers to create a personally valued adult lifestyle will greatly contribute to their future happiness and well-being. There are defining moments in teenagers' lives when they take a step toward becoming who they really want to be. This book will help you help your teenager take these steps.

• Game Plan •

This book is not about your teenagers prematurely deciding on the "right" career choice. This will evolve as they mature. This book is about motivating your adolescents to become actively engaged in exploring career and educational pathways that will increase their success and happiness in the present and future. The best way to do this is for you to get actively involved and do it with them. You have too much at stake not to take a very active part.

This book will take you through a *TEAM!* process grounded in the best available research on adolescent development. You will learn which behavioral *T*argets to focus in on. You will be introduced to real-life *E*xamples of 12th graders, some who have mastered and some still struggling to reach these targets. You will be shown how to *A*ssess your child's development of these critical behavioral targets. You will be provided activities that you can *M*utually do together with your adolescent. And finally, you and your teenager will construct an effective educational and career transition plan!

The activities that you will do will show you and your teenager strategies for using the enormous resources *freely* available on the Internet. For example, you will search for the right college for your adolescent, find out what it is likely to cost, plan for how your family is going to pay for college, and learn how your child could one day start his or her own business. By the end of this book, both you and your teenager will know how to use freely available online resources for whatever educational and career planning adventures you both may want to undertake. You will practice more effective communication styles, so you can more successfully listen and speak to your teenager about these life-altering decisions. These are truly lifelong skills that will be of great value to your teenager across her or his life span.

This book will take you step by step through a process that will be of great benefit to your teenager. The rewards for doing this are huge. In the years to come, the personal and financial costs to your children and your family for not doing this will continue to skyrocket. Let's get started!

• Part One •
Warm-Ups

• Chapter 1 •
What Dreams Will Your Teenagers Seek?

This chapter congratulates you for the hard work you have already put in to be a good parent. To mention a few things, you have helped your kids learn how to walk, read, ride a bike, and make friends. A big part of your concern has been to get them ready to live as happy, productive, and responsible adults. It is now time to support their efforts to create a meaningful and satisfying place in the work world. Most parents whose children are grown talk about how fast the time sped by. Your children will be graduating from high school before you know it. Helping them bridge the transition between adolescence and young adulthood is an invaluable parental gift.

• Career Development: Why Now? •

I am a parent of three daughters (now 22, 19, and 17). Each is unique in her talents, temperament, personality, motivations, and values. If we came to your house for a party, except for the fact that we had just arrived together, you would find it difficult to pick out which three belonged to me. They have distinctive looks, conversational styles, comfort levels around others, television shows they like, books they read, and even sleep patterns. One always put herself to sleep by 9:30 p.m.; another is a night owl who needed clear directives to shut things down and go to bed. When my oldest daughter was about 11 she said to me, "Daddy, when you get old, I will stay home and take care of you." Upon hearing this, her then 8-year-old sister said, "Daddy, I'm going to be a lawyer, so when you get old, I will send you money."

One of our daughters has significant special needs that have made us all too familiar with speech and language therapists, special education teachers, an assortment of medical specialists, as well as EEG and MRI machines. Our oldest daughter is very kind to people and never says a bad word about anybody (except her sisters at times). She is great at remembering specific details and procedures that need to be followed. She is the only one in the family who can spell something correctly. My middle daughter is very good at math, fixing things, and debate. She has talked about becoming a lawyer ever since she was able to object that she should be allowed to do something that we said she couldn't. Our youngest has some real art talent. Her drawings have won awards, drawn positive comment and recognition, and won a $100 gift certificate that I got to spend! With her mother and sisters, she loves to help paint and design the sets for a local children's theater group. When she was about 15, I asked her if she thought that someday she might use her art talents in a career. She looked at me without hesitation and said, "Well, you know Dad, you can't get a good job doing art." Stupefied and thinking about the world of computer animation as well as the importance of art in every aspect of our lives, I couldn't think of anything else to say but "What! Who ever told you that?"

You can see her entry in the "Draw Your Dad" contest in Figure 1.1. She got a kick out of giving me our dog Oskar's tongue. I spent most of the prize money buying a frame for the picture. She drew the picture for the cover of this book. I hope you like it. It means a lot to me to have her picture there.

• Figure 1.1 •
Dad, Richard Lapan

Artist: Kaylin Lapan, age 12.

I have just written an academic book that integrates the current research literature on the career development of children, adolescents, and young adults. From this perspective, I can honestly say to you that I have no idea what the "right" career for each of my daughters would be. In fact, I don't believe there is one right career for each of them. Rather, they are each beginning to take different paths that will lead them to a range of good choices. It is going to be up to them to hammer out a career that means something vital in their lives.

I hope I never hear one of them say something like, "Well, you know Dad, I really hate what I am doing but the money is just too good to walk away from." Maybe leisure activities could round out their lives, but for most people satisfaction with their career is an important part of the satisfaction they find in their lives, the quality of their health, and even the success of their marriage. In fact, researchers have found that on average people live about 7½ years longer if they find that their lives in retirement have worth, meaning, and purpose (Levy, Slade, Kunkel, & Kasl, 2002). I hope my daughters find these qualities in their everyday, adult work lives.

This book will help you engage your children in an in-depth exploration of these critical life questions. The exercises in Part Two provide you with a foundation to identify strengths and areas of concern that should be improved before your teenagers graduate from high school. The challenges of important transitions come much quicker than we like or ever think will happen. Your eighth grader will soon have to choose electives and high school courses. Your high school junior could benefit from a career direction that begins to make some coursework relevant to her or his future. Graduating from a postsecondary educational or career-technical training program is now a necessity for a young person to successfully enter a high-skill, high-wage career.

Your teenagers will face these decisions whether they are ready to make them or not. Too many young people struggle in college to find a major that really fits them (talk to some parents who are paying thousands of dollars of college tuition for credits that they painfully realize are leading their career-undecided son or daughter in circles). Too many young adults have very little self-understanding. When a young person has little insight into who she or he is (including values, interests, talents, and goals), it is unlikely that this person will make good educational and career decisions. Right now, you can help your teenager learn how to do this.

• High School Will Soon Be Over, What's Next for Your Teenager? •

When asked by her school counselor about what she hoped her future career would be like, a high school senior replied, "I'd like to have something that I really enjoy and can get wrapped up into. I want something that I can get up and want to go to work for. I'd want to affect people in a positive way."

Ready or not, high school is over and this young woman has reached the edge of a life-altering transition. She has sort of identified an educational direction that she will pursue after graduation. She has an idea of the kind of person she would like to become. She is imagining a particular kind of adult lifestyle she would enjoy having. She is aware of certain values that are important for her to express in her work. Above all, she is very hopeful and optimistic about her future.

Intuitively, this young woman knows that her life will be less urgent, less vital, and much less interesting if she does not find her way into a career in which she will do things that really mean something to her. It goes against everything positive in her nature to think that one day she could be trapped in a job that is devoid of meaning, purpose, and self-expression. She correctly senses that her well-being in adulthood will be greatly improved if she is fortunate enough to be employed in a career that adds direction, significance, and self-fulfillment to her life.

As adults, we know at least two things about her journey. First, she will be confronted by numerous challenges and opportunities. Some of these she can plan for, but many will happen completely by chance. She will face the inevitability of having to make difficult career transitions, deal with job loss, and ride out the ups and downs of large-scale economic trends. This young woman may one day want to have children of her own. She and her partner will then have to work hard to create a satisfying pattern for their lives. Her happiness, well-being, and overall satisfaction in life will depend on their combined efforts to successfully harmonize their multiple roles (such as child-care provider, worker, spousal partner, and citizen) if life in this family is going to be generative, imaginative, and fulfilling.

Unpredictable events will present this young woman with new opportunities and new hurdles. For example, who could have known that the Internet would so completely change our lives? It even caught Bill Gates by surprise. But as Louis Pasteur once said, "Chance events favor the prepared mind." Is this young woman prepared to deal with the ups, downs, changes, and curves that adult life will soon throw at her? If you were her parent, what would you do to help her to be better prepared? What are you doing right now for your own children?

Second, to carelessly give up one's dreams can lead to much unhappiness in life. To have talents that are never expressed is an all too frequent occurrence. One of the most famous studies in my field found that highly gifted women who had not used their unique talents experienced many more mental health problems later in their lives (Sears & Barbie, 1977). You probably know someone who graduated from high school with a range of interests and talents (just like this young woman) but by the time that person reached 35 or 40 he or she had given up and settled for something much less satisfying—leaving you puzzled and wondering why his or her potential went unrealized.

• Conclusion •

In my counseling work I have witnessed the depressing effects that career settling and compromising can have on one's life: doors that have been closed or, worse yet, openings that were never attempted; lives that have become one dimensional and dreadfully repetitive; adults who feel that there is no spark, no magic, and certainly no passion in their daily lives. However, I have also seen the resurgence of energy and enthusiasm that animate people when new attempts are made to pursue a discarded or forgotten career path. Hopefulness and joy follow from the active pursuit of meaningful life projects. *What dreams will your teenagers seek?*

• Chapter 2 •
Parental Involvement—The Best Medicine

To empower your teenagers to be successful, you have to be actively involved in their lives. Adolescence is not the time to disengage and act like your job as a parent is over. This chapter presents a brief overview of a collaborative teamwork strategy that I will help you put in place with your teenagers.

• Teams Work •

Imagine that your youngest child is now 30 years old. What would that make you? I'm sorry, don't answer that. What do you hope your child's life is like by then? If you really want your child to still be living in your basement and not paying rent, stop reading this book immediately and see if you can get your money back.

Parental involvement has been found to be the necessary antidote for the big issues that threaten our young people today. To stop children from using drugs, parents must dare to insert themselves into their children's lives and make a big deal about it. The best way to prevent your children from smoking cigarettes is to talk to them. I am daring you to deeply engage your middle school, junior high, and high school children (and maybe especially your "grown up" college student) in a series of conversations, joint activities, and career planning exercises. Right now, one of the best things that you can do for your teenagers is to help them initiate a serious exploration of the pathways that lead to greater success and career satisfaction in young adulthood. Sooner than all of you think, pivotal educational and career decisions will have to be made. It is not my goal to raise your or your teenagers' level of anxiety about the road ahead. Instead, we will work together to promote your teenagers' ability to act in the present and move toward the future with a greater sense of hopefulness, purpose, and direction.

In every arena, teamwork is a necessary ingredient for success. Great teams use collaboration to achieve outcomes that go well beyond anything that one individual could accomplish alone. The whole becomes greater than the sum of its individual parts. I learned this from watching the Boston Celtics and listening to my first real hero, Bill Russell. Bill Russell led the Celtics to 11 championships in 13 years. Known for his revolutionary defensive skills, Russell was the brain that enabled the Celtics to be great. I will always remember one interview in which Russell revealed his understanding of his teammates' psyches and how he kept them engaged in the game. Russell was aware of when a teammate was drifting, not really making a full contribution, and he used his control of the basketball in the high post to engage his teammates. He did this by passing the ball, setting up his teammates so that they could get their shots. If you have ever played any team sports, then you know how motivating this can be. With Russell as the hub that kept the collaboration flowing, the Celtics functioned at a higher level of efficiency for longer periods of time than anyone had ever done. The Celtics achieved unparalleled success, becoming known for their trademark unselfish passing and teamwork.

• TEAM! •
(Targets + Examples + Assessments + Mutual Actions = Success!)

Listen to any CEO, manager, or innovator talk about success and you will hear talk about teamwork. By forming a special kind of collaborative alliance and teamwork with your daughter or son, you can play a pivotal role in preparing your teenager to more successfully cope with future occupational realities. To help you engage your children in this collaborative process of exploration and self-definition, we will follow a five-step strategy.

First, you will read about the seven building blocks (*T*argets) that your children need if they are to develop a proactive, resilient, and adaptive orientation to the present and their career futures. Second, you will meet successful 12th graders (*E*xamples) who are working to make these targets a part of their lives. Third, through the Structured Career Development Interview you will measure how well your teenagers are making these targets come to life in their world at school, with their friends, and at home (*A*ssessments). Fourth, after talking to your teenagers about their hopes and dreams, you will work together on exercises that will enhance your children's understanding of themselves and their options after they leave high school (*M*utual actions). Fifth, together, you and your son or daughter will develop an educational and career plan (Success*!*).

• Conclusion •

Throughout this book you will do activities with your teenagers to help them discover how each of the critical skills covered in our *TEAM!* work can become a potent force in how they more fully engage in school, with their friends, and at home, and how they are trying to achieve a future they really value. Together, we will put your teenagers in the driver's seat when making decisions about what they will do and where they will go after high school. But first, the best way to stay connected with your teenagers is to establish good communication patterns with them. Chapter 3 will help you to do this.

• Chapter 3 •
If You Listen, They Will Talk; If You Lecture, They Will Walk

This chapter briefly discusses critical communication skills that will help you to engage your teenagers in *TEAM!* work about their futures. Ten strategies to use when talking to your children are identified, and more complete descriptions of these techniques are included in the Appendix. Please pay close attention and learn how to develop career-related I-messages. You will use this skill when presenting the results of the Structured Career Development Interview to your teenagers. Career-related I-messages are so important that information on using this communication strategy is provided both in this chapter and in the Appendix. The chapter concludes with an overview of what not to do in a conversation with your teenagers about their future educational and career plans.

• If You Listen, They Will Talk •

Counseling works because open communication is encouraged among everyone involved. Certain kinds of communication patterns lead to closer emotional bonds forged in trust, caring, support, mutuality, cooperation, and attachment. Agreement is reached on the goals to be realized and the strategies that will enable these goals to be successfully achieved. Effective and open communication will help to motivate your son or daughter to become an active collaborator with you as you work together in a series of career exploration, planning, and decision-making activities. My goal is to help you engage your teenager in a process of exploration and goal formation that will enable your teenager to define her or his own ideas about the future. In this way, your son or daughter will begin the process of creating his or her own career direction and thus make progress in resolving the identity challenges of adolescence. To do this, you will need to engage your teenager as an active, reflective partner. The best way to make this happen is to embrace your daughter or son in meaningful conversations. I encourage you to thoroughly familiarize yourself with the 10 communication strategies described in this chapter, and make sure you routinely use these techniques. The success of so much of what you are trying to accomplish depends on the kinds of communication practices that are routinely used in your family.

Getting your teenagers to talk to you about their career development is relatively easy. While the stereotype of adolescence portrays teenagers as being closed off and uncommunicative with their parents, talking to them about their future career aspirations should not pose such a problem. Okay, I am going out on a bit of a limb here, but let me explain. When asked to identify the most important issues in their lives, teenagers have repeatedly said that they want help with their career planning and decision making and would like to talk to someone about these things (Lapan, 2004).

So, the very first thing you must do is to develop a strong positive belief (have the self-confidence) that your adolescents want to talk to you about their future hopes and dreams. For the past several years, I have used the approach presented in this book with high school sophomores (some of whom were having tough times in school and could be very oppositional). Many of these students were not very motivated about school and got their backs up about requests that came from adults.

Using the communication strategies you will learn here, I have had very good success getting these students to open up by focusing on their career issues.

Careers are part of that positive motivational reservoir that we all would like to swim in. Careers are endpoints that signify to adolescents valued, desirable lifestyles that could one day be theirs. In my experience, even the most resistant and oppositional teenagers will give you a chance to connect with them around issues relevant to their future. This is mission possible (and I hope you choose to accept this assignment).

Effective communication with your teenagers about their career dreams is all about style. It's all in how you go about doing it. You need to consistently use a few deceptively simple listening skills. Remember, when it comes to communicating with your teenagers—keep it simple—short and sweet wins the race.

Your goal is to initiate and then sustain a conversation with your teenagers about their career aspirations. In the assessment section of this book, I describe questions to ask, types of responses you should make, how to score their answers to your questions, how to interpret the results to your teenagers, and joint activities to do to move their career identity development forward.

Your job is to listen and learn. You will need to understand your teen's perspective on these critical issues. By listening, you will gather information to assess how your child is developing important career development skills. We will work together to help your child. Your empathic involvement in your teenager's life will let your child know, in no uncertain terms, that she or he is not alone in facing one of the central challenges of her or his life.

To improve your chances that your teenagers will talk to you, use the "Top 10 Tips for Talking to Your Teenagers" outlined in Box 3.1. Human conversation is really an incredibly wonderful thing.

• Box 3.1 •

Top 10 Tips for Talking to Your Teenagers

1. *Pay attention to the environment.* Carefully choose the right setting and the right time for a conversation.
2. *Pay attention to yourself.* What is your body language saying? Are you really telling your teenagers you want to talk with them?
3. *Use communication encouragers.* Smiles and head nods are good encouragers; it's the little things that encourage your teenagers to keep talking.
4. *Restate what you have heard.* Every so often, put into words what you think your teenagers are trying to communicate. Listening is hard work; make sure you understand what your children are trying to say.
5. *Use open-ended questions.* Some questions can shut down a conversation; open-ended questions encourage mutual problem solving and collaboration.
6. *Use reflections of feelings and content.* Be an empathic listener, and hear your teenagers' perspectives and their feelings.
7. *Make helpful interpretations.* Don't try to be a know-it-all, but look for important patterns and themes in what your children are saying.
8. *Appropriately disclose personal information.* Recounting both the good events and the difficult things you have faced in your life can help your teenagers better see their path and their challenges.
9. *Be emotionally intimate with your child.* It really is okay to let your adolescent know who you are.
10. *Use career-related I-messages.* When expressing your point of view, address behavior, feelings, and consequences. Because this is so important, instructions and examples are provided in this chapter.

Think of a time when you were troubled by something. If you kept it to yourself and tried to figure it out, how far did you get? How much more confused and unsettled did you feel because you hung onto your feelings and kept them rather selfishly to yourself? There is something about sharing yourself, your thoughts and feelings, with another human being that is healing, empowering, and rejuvenating.

Tip 10. Career-Related I-Messages

You will be using career-related I-messages to speak to your teenagers about their assessment results, so I have included a discussion of this very valuable communication strategy here. In the effective parenting literature, Dinkmeyer, McKay, and Dinkmeyer (1997) recommended that parents use I-messages to clearly and assertively communicate their point of view to their children. First, the parent tells their child about the specific behaviors the child has performed that are a cause of concern or joy for the parent. These are events that have real consequences (either positive or negative) for the parent and child. Then, the parent identifies the feelings he or she has about these consequences. And finally, the parent clearly points out what the consequences of the events or actions taken by the child are. Dinkmeyer et al. recommended a three-part structure (behavior, feelings, consequences), which I have adapted to help our work. To more effectively get your point across when speaking to your teenagers about their career development, use empowering I-messages. The structure of I-messages is as follows:

When _____ → I feel _____ → because _____ .

Here are two examples.

A. *When* you don't really take our conversation seriously about what high school courses you will sign up for next year, *I feel* worried *because* you may miss out on some great opportunities.
B. *When* you decided just now to take the pre-calculus class, *I felt* very good *because* it showed me that you weren't going to back away from a difficult challenge.

Remember, you can use career-related I-messages to emphasize things that are troubling to you as well as actions performed by your teenagers that you think are quite wonderful and exciting. Throughout this book you will be given additional training and have opportunities to construct career-related I-messages that effectively express your feelings and ideas to your children.

• If You Lecture, They Will Walk •

What not to do! There are a lot of different ways to be a good parent. We see evidence of this in how diverse ethnic, cultural, and racial groups effectively love, nurture, and raise their children. But we also clearly see that there are definitely some destructive ways to be a parent. For example, not confronting your children when they have stumbled into using illegal drugs is bad parenting policy. Like parenting, there are many good and diverse ways to promote intimate conversations with your children. As well, there are actions you can take that will destroy a conversation with your children faster than a politician can smile on Election Day.

Here are some of the main culprits that ruin communication between parents and their teenagers. First of all, please remember, listening is hard work. Don't be so quick to give advice. Avoid criticisms, evaluative statements, and judgments. Watch your body language. Get rid of distracters, such as tapping a pen or sneaking a quick peek at the television or looking at the newspaper out of the corner of your eye. Don't be desperate to make everything happen at once.

A good conversation with your teenager about their educational and career goals takes some time, and you both have a stake in it. If it doesn't go well the first time, try again later, at a better time and place. This is likely to be the first time anyone has attempted to have a serious conversation with your teenager about such issues. Given where your child is developmentally, it is normal for your teenager to look a little dazed, lost, confused, frightened, or slightly irritated when you start your first conversation about colleges she or he might like to attend.

Don't ask "why" questions; they tend to make the speaker feel a bit self-conscious and unsure of what to say. "Why" questions can shut off sharing and exploration. Closed responses such as "Why don't you forget about it, this isn't a big deal" communicate to your teenager that you don't want to connect or understand. Open responses such as "You're still pretty upset about this" let your teenager know that you understand and are with him or her. Open responses give your teenager a green light to proceed with further exploration, and such statements let your child know that you will continue to be engaged as he or she does this important task.

Like fingerprints, each of us has our own unique style of communicating. Be aware of your own personal quirks or habits that might stop an intimate conversation from happening with your child. Finally, remember to go on your child's time.

• Conclusion •

You will use these communication skills to complete the *TEAM!* work activities that will propel your teenagers' development toward careers that are both personally satisfying and a meaningful expression of the adults they want to become.

• Part Two •
TEAM! for Success

• Chapter 4 •
Targets

• Target 1 •
Help Your Teenagers Become Proactive, Resilient, and Adaptive Adults

This target outlines three strengths that your teenagers need if they are going to be successful in a radically changing work world. First, it is an advantage if your children can size up situations and chart independent courses of action (be proactive). Second, young adults who can bounce back from adversity will be better prepared for the challenges that they will inevitably face (be resilient). Third, women and men who develop career plans based on significant exploratory behaviors will better understand themselves and be more likely to find valued goals and a direction to which they can enthusiastically commit themselves (be adaptive; Blustein, 2006; Lapan, Aoyagi, & Kayson, 2007).

Proactivity, Resilience, and Adaptability

A couple of years ago, my oldest friend lost a job he had held with the same company for the past 25 years. He is a highly competent engineer, whose work on sophisticated defense systems regularly earned him great performance reviews and pay raises. But at 54 and with the economy struggling, he became expendable. Younger people are much cheaper. His son had just become part owner in a small business, and my friend's wife was working closely with their son to make the new business a success. He and his wife, adult son, and daughter (who was finishing a doctorate in humanities at a university not too far from where they lived) faced a radically life-altering challenge. In his first attempt to resolve this crisis, my friend took a job similar to the one he had held for most of his working career. However, this meant that he had to live in the city where this new job was (about 8 hours away by car) and visit home on the weekends. As you can imagine, this was no way to live.

To my friend's credit, he then reinvented himself. Realizing that he needed to be at home and get a job with a reasonable daily commute, he expanded his search to engineering positions he hadn't really considered before. In his explorations, he came across a job with a company that specialized in producing pictures taken from satellites. Now that lit his imagination and connected him to activities that he had loved when he was in school. It meant a bit of a pay cut in the short term, but it was more than enough to maintain the satisfying life pattern their family had created. He is now enjoying this job, and it takes him only 45 minutes to drive to work. As a result, he and his family have been able to maintain (in a community of their choosing) a valued lifestyle that took them almost 3 decades to put in place.

My guess is that my friend's situation is not all that different from work challenges you or someone you know has had to face. Intuitively, you are keenly aware that to be successful in the economy of today and tomorrow it is a real advantage to be proactive, resilient, and adaptive.

Okay, that is a mouthful. Let me explain. Being proactive means that you can initiate actions that anticipate important events and act in your own best interest. Resilient people bounce back from adversity and learn from their experiences. Adaptive individuals adjust their behavior to better cope with the pressing demands of everyday situations. It is essential that your teenagers integrate a proactive, resilient, and adaptive style of acting in the present and move toward career futures that they highly value. To better understand how to interact with the world from this foundation of strength, let's look at each of these factors in more depth.

Proactivity. The work world your teenagers will enter rewards those who can act with forethought to anticipate short- and long-term opportunities. Initiative and assertiveness, combined with an ability to make decisions and act in one's own best interest, are necessary counterweights to current realities such as corporate downsizing, job loss, and the bygone era of secure lifetime employment with a single company.

I am not saying that your teenagers need to become selfish, but they do need to learn how to be their own agent. When necessary, can they be a director who can chart an independent course of action? With each career step they take, new opportunities will open up. From the myriad choices available to them, a willingness to commit to, engage in, and entrust a part of themselves to a particular direction is required. Hopeful and motivated adults who optimistically expect the best outcomes to follow from their efforts will do better. Individuals who create and have an inner desire to learn, investigate, and explore will be more highly valued. People who can take risks and make their own jobs are on their way toward becoming successful entrepreneurs.

Resilience. Recovery from misfortune, the ability to bounce back from events that stretch and bend us, gives us the determination to stay on those difficult paths that lead to the attainment of valued goals. Being resolute and even a little tenacious balances off daily ups and downs and enables adults to better cope with economic trends over which they have no real control. Persistence, perseverance, and a touch of stubbornness can cut problems down into more manageable bites.

Adversity confronts everyone. Advantages accrue to those who can cope with and seize the opportunities made available by events and tasks that challenge us. To follow their dreams, your teenagers will have to open many doors. Over time they will discover that both positive and negative outcomes may await them on the other side. Can they recoup from wrong turns, dead ends, and failure? Can they pull themselves back together and keep moving forward when things don't go their way?

Adaptability. Relating to others and the environment with a sense of balance and harmony nurtures inner peace, calmness, and self-confidence. Such a focus follows from a life that has found purpose and a positive direction. Such a life has meaning and reason. This helps us move toward the future with intention and design. Careful consideration and planning encourage a maturity to commit oneself to the pursuit of valued goals. Exploration leads to self-understanding and goals that express this self-knowledge. A world striving to shed itself of petty divisions, old hatreds, and racial exploitations will reward those who embrace human diversity, are empathic toward others, and act within a framework that safeguards the fragile ecosystems we need to survive.

Conclusion

Your teenagers' chances of becoming proactive, resilient, and adaptive young adults will be greatly improved if they can do six things. They need to have self-confidence, develop effective goals, understand themselves, be able to pursue their interests, become self-directed lifelong learners, and get along well with others. Each of these strengths is a targeted skill that you can help your children learn.

• Target 2 •
Help Your Teenagers Believe in Themselves

This target focuses on the kinds of self-efficacy beliefs (Bandura, 1997) and attributions (Weiner, 1986) that will help your teenagers believe in themselves. In the United States, freedom is one of our most cherished political and economic values. It is a cornerstone for how we expect successful adults to establish themselves in productive careers. If you can exert some degree of self-direction over the course your life will take, you are much more likely to find your way into a career in which you will be successful and personally fulfilled. The beliefs your children hold play a key role in their ability to be free, self-determining adults. The success that they experience when considering career possibilities, charting a self-determined course of action, and coping with adversity is dependent upon these beliefs. Certain kinds of expectations empower children to successfully reach short- and long-range goals. Your teenagers' ability to be proactive, resilient, and adaptive in creating careers that they really value is made possible by the self-efficacy beliefs they hold and the attribution styles they use to realize their dreams.

Self-Efficacy Beliefs and Outcome Expectations

"Can I do this?" Every day your children are confronted with challenges and opportunities. These encounters require them to adapt, cope, or excel if they are to be successful. The noted researcher Albert Bandura (1997) found that our ability to cope with challenging or threatening situations has a great deal to do with our own self-assessment of how competent we feel ourselves to be to perform the tasks required for success in that specific situation. For example, regardless of their level of ability or potential, if teenagers do not believe they can learn how to solve difficult math problems, they will be much less likely to want to take math classes. If they try taking a college algebra class, they will be at risk for not persevering when they confront obstacles with the material or the teacher. Research has found that students with the ability to be successful will engage in self-defeating behaviors that destroy their chances for success if they do not believe that they are capable of performing the tasks required for success in that specific learning situation (Jacobs, 1991).

Your teenagers make these kinds of assessments of their own competence in every situation they are in. Self-efficacy judgments are a primary means by which they tell themselves whether they are competent to successfully perform a wide range of actions. For example, efficacy judgments are involved when estimating whether or not they can solve the trigonometry problems that have been assigned for homework, their self-confidence in being able to successfully plan for their future, or their perceived ability to be a successful public speaker.

Career development is greatly influenced by these self-assessments of personal competence. Your teenagers' choice of, persistence in, and success in a nontraditional career—such as a young woman entering a math, science, and technology-related career like engineering or computer science, or a young man who wants to go into nursing—are greatly helped or hindered by the self-efficacy beliefs they hold about these possible futures (Lent, Brown, & Hackett, 1994; Multon, Brown, & Lent, 1991).

"If I do this, what will I get out of it?" Working in tandem with self-efficacy beliefs, outcome expectations identify the consequences that are likely to happen should your teenagers follow a certain path. For example, your teenagers may believe they can be successful in the chemistry classes offered at their high school. However, they may not believe it is very likely that even if they passed every difficult chemistry course with a good grade they could become successful chemists working in private industry. They do not believe that a good outcome will follow as a result of being successful in these courses. If your teenagers do not see the possibility of positive rewards that follow from their success (like earning more money, gaining your approval, or achieving self-satisfaction), they will be much less motivated to pursue a particular course of action. If they don't see that it will pay off for them, they will not be motivated to go after it.

How Do Teenagers Learn What Kind of Self-Assessments to Make?

They learn it from others. Bandura (1977) demonstrated that we gather the information we use to make these judgments of perceived competence and anticipated outcomes from four primary sources of learning.

1. *Mastery experiences:* your child actually performs a task successfully
2. *Modeling:* your child learns by observing and watching others

3. *Social persuasion:* others talk your child into or out of believing in his or her competence
4. *Mood states:* for example, your child becomes anxious and infers that this is a situation and task that he or she is not competent to perform

As it turns out, these are the conduits through which you can enhance the judgments that your teenagers make about themselves. Box 4.1 presents brief definitions and examples of the types of efficacy and outcome expectations that you might hear your teenagers talk about.

Attribution Styles

Every day, your teenagers interact with others in a complex web of tasks and situations. Some of their efforts will succeed, whereas others will not work out for them. Your teenagers are innately predisposed and motivated to interpret the reasons one thing was a success while another was a complete failure. They will try to identify the causes of their successes and failures. To do this, your teenagers will use a lot of different factors to explain to themselves why things happened as they did. They might tell themselves that they succeeded because of their natural talents and abilities, or the effort and hard work they put in. Your teenagers will also look to see if any luck was involved, what kind of mood they were in during the interaction, and whether or not others helped or hindered their success.

Conversely, they might interpret their failure as being due to their lack of ability, talent, and effort. The way they choose to do this is very important. For example, some studies have found that women are more likely than men to interpret failure as being due to internal factors such as a lack of ability, whereas men are more likely to blame their failure on factors outside of themselves

• Box 4.1 •

Efficacy Expectations and Attributions

Belief	*Definition*	*Example*
Efficacy expectations	They are or are not capable of successfully performing a specific task.	"I am very confident that I can correctly solve this quadratic equation."
Outcome expectations	If they engage in specific activities, they will obtain certain rewards or outcomes in the more distant future.	"If I take extra science and mathematics courses in high school, I will be much better prepared to enter a 2-year engineering technician program that pays great."
Locus attributions	The cause of an event is either internal or external to them.	"I got a B on my last physics test because I worked extra hard to be prepared, and for the first time I did all the practice homework problems."
Stability attributions	The cause of an event may or may not change over time.	"My parents are never going to be able to afford to pay $25,000 a year for my college tuition."
Control attributions	The cause of an event is something they can either influence or not be able to do anything about.	"I'm smart enough to get good grades in these mathematics and science courses. That is not going to change. I have control over how well I do." (optimistic attribution style)

(Graham, 1991). I recently heard one of the best women's college soccer coaches speak. He had an intuitive understanding of this dynamic and talked about the different motivational approaches he needed to use to be successful with his women's team that were markedly different from how he had coached college soccer for men. His women players were quick to blame failure on themselves, whereas the men easily found ways to point the finger somewhere else.

The well-known researcher Bernard Weiner (1986) clearly laid out how each cause that we attribute as an explanation for why we succeed or fail is constructed on top of a three-legged foundation:

Locus: whether the cause of the event is internal or external to the person
Stability: whether the cause is likely to change over time
Control: whether the cause can be changed by anything that the person can do

The attributions your teenagers make play a big role in constructing the reality that they find around them. Barriers to career futures (e.g., the financial costs of college) can be seen as permanent roadblocks or problems that can be successfully managed. Here is a brief example to help you see how locus, stability, and control attributions can influence how teenagers interpret barriers to their educational and career development.

Alan is a Caucasian American 11th grader who attends a suburban high school. He is a very strong student. Having gotten very good grades in difficult honors courses, Alan ranks in the top 10% of a class of almost 600 students. During our interview, he was very upbeat until he was asked to describe future barriers and challenges to his educational and career development. He said:

> Okay. The challenges will probably be that my mom's a single parent and that my dad passed away last year, so it'd be like getting money from one income, and my job's just not enough to pay for college, but if I start early and look for scholarships then it should. I should be okay. Financial aid, I mean like we can always get loans. Another thing is that my older sister has a kid, so we pay . . . my mom supports that too, so that's hard.

At first Alan spoke optimistically about a range of interesting options that he saw for himself. However, when thinking about the significant financial problems threatening his educational aspirations, his mood became markedly pessimistic, hesitant, and downcast. The death of his father has had dramatic and unexpected ramifications for Alan's career development. A year later, he was beginning to interpret the financial implications of his father's death as a permanent roadblock that could stop him dead in his tracks from ever achieving his "A-list" educational and career dreams. He was beginning to believe that he would have to settle for something much less than he had anticipated as a very successful high school sophomore. Alan was now coming to understand the issue of financial aid as a cause that was external to him, a permanent barrier that was not going to change. This was a situation over which he could not see any way of exerting personal control.

Alan's school counselor was concerned that Alan had almost given up on the top choices for colleges he had been considering before his father's death. He was compromising and limiting his future horizons to fall in line with a situation over which he did not see that he had any personal control and believed was not going to change. Even though Alan's overall sense of self-esteem appeared strong, this more pessimistic attribution about financial aid was now limiting the possibilities he saw for himself (eliminating choices that he was highly qualified to pursue). When young people like Alan find themselves thinking their way into dead ends, it is up to parents, teachers, and school counselors to provide the support needed to find solutions to these barriers and not allow our children to give up on their valued dreams.

Box 4.1 also provides examples of locus, stability, and control attributions that your teenagers are likely to make. If your teenagers consistently employ an optimistic attribution style, they will very likely be experiencing significant advantages right now that will greatly assist them when they enter the workforce. An optimistic attribution style interprets the causes of career-related events to be due to internal, controllable, and unstable factors. If your teenagers feel that they have some degree of control and responsibility for the decisions they have to make and the barriers they have to face, they will be more decisive, engage in a more serious exploration of their options, be more likely to commit to a productive career direction, and hold higher career aspirations and achievement goals for themselves (Luzzo & Jenkins-Smith, 1998).

Adults who use a more optimistic attribution style are more likely to find jobs that match their aspirations, be more satisfied with their jobs, perform better on the job, and have greater tenure in their job (Luzzo & Ward, 1995). College students (both at 2- and 4-year institutions) who use a positive attribution style have similar advantages. Barriers are not seen as permanent roadblocks. Your daughter or son will see challenges as opportunities she or he can successfully handle and maybe even profit from.

Parents Shape Their Teenagers' Expectations and Attribution Styles

If you believe your teenagers can be competent at a task or in a certain situation, they will be much more likely to believe it themselves. Parental support, encouragement, and affirmation are fundamental building blocks that help young people believe in their capabilities, that good things follow from their efforts, and that they will be able to successfully handle the challenges they face. If you believe in your children, they will see challenges as exciting new possibilities for learning and growth.

Your beliefs about your teenagers' areas of competence can either positively enhance or negatively distort their own understanding of themselves. For example, researchers have found that mothers who believe in certain traditional gender-role stereotypes (such as that math is both harder and less important for their daughters' future than for their sons' future) have daughters who greatly underestimate their own ability to do mathematics (Jacobs & Eccles, 1992). Even though the young women in this study were very competently performing in their math classes (at a rate and pace at least equal to their male peers), they nevertheless believed they were not as competent to successfully perform in this domain. Their lowered efficacy expectations mirrored the gender-role beliefs of their mothers.

Such a lowered sense of self-competence can derail the pursuit of careers that involve math, science, and technology (engineer, computer systems analyst, or research chemist, to name just a few). The tendency to align one's perceptions of competence to prevailing societal and family perceptions is so strong that it can occur even in the face of strong contradictory evidence. Parental support can make all the difference in the world in convincing your teenagers of their self-competence in the face of the unknowns that await them as they move into young adulthood. It is definitely worth your time to talk to your kids about these issues.

Conclusion

This target focused on two critical strengths that greatly influence whether or not your teenagers will believe in themselves. We want to help young people develop strong efficacy expectations and an optimistic attribution style. Parents play a key role in helping their children develop these qualities and skills. The Structured Career Development Interview that you will learn about in Chapter 6 will help you to talk to your teenagers about these critical strengths.

• Target 3 •
Help Your Teenagers Create Effective Educational and Career Goals

This target will help you better understand the career identity development opportunities your children have in adolescence and young adulthood. To thrive, young people should engage in an extensive exploration of educational and career choices, develop effective goals linked to this exploration process, and then move toward committing themselves to a self-chosen career direction. Reflect on the ways your teenagers are coping with the career identity development opportunity that is now before them. Do they seem confused? Would they be likely to let others solve this problem for them? Or are they seriously engaged in an active process of exploration to gather the information needed to make such important decisions?

Resolving the Identity Crisis in Adolescence

My daughters have now hit the many different phases of adolescence, some compassion for the parents please! My oldest daughter has left her teenage years. She voted with us in the last presidential election. She gathered information about her favorite candidates and put pressure on me to vote the same way she did. As a high school junior, my middle daughter claimed ownership over one of the family cars. Like a Doberman sitting on its owner's front lawn, she was ever ready to defend her turf. Her then 15-year-old sister got a big laugh out of undoing her big sister's attempts at power and domination. During most of these days I felt very blessed. But at the close of some, I felt the kind of thankfulness you have when in your 50s you reach the end of a very long roller coaster ride.

I can see in each of my daughters the child and the newly emerging adult. Both forms trapped together, at the same time, in the same body. Awkward at times, sleek and graceful at others, I often catch a glimpse of an adult face staring out at me. No wonder adolescents are confused and often feel overwhelmed. In so many ways the challenge of adolescence is to create a bridge the child can cross over to become the young adult. This is the challenge of identity development in adolescence. During these years, the question "Who am I?" demands attention and some beginning answers. An important part of the solution to this puzzle comes from the successful development of a career identity that adds purpose, direction, focus, and hope to your child's life.

To fully take possession of their lives, adolescents need to create a career identity for themselves. To do this, they will need to become actively engaged in two interlocking processes—career exploration and goal formation (Flum & Blustein, 2000). From the interplay between exploration and goal formation, your teenagers will construct a proactive orientation toward the future that will commit them to a productive course of action (see Figure 4.1). Learning how to do this will give your children adaptive advantages across their life span. Respected researchers have found that such skills enhance well-being and satisfaction in adulthood and assist individuals in creating meaning across the changing tasks and stages of their life span (Robbins & Kliewer, 2000; Savickas, 1997).

Career Exploration

Your teenagers will have resolved the identity crisis of adolescence (Erikson, 1968) as they assert themselves as the "authors of their own becoming" (Flum & Blustein, 2000, p. 386). They need to construct for themselves a direction toward the future. This path is autonomously chosen and

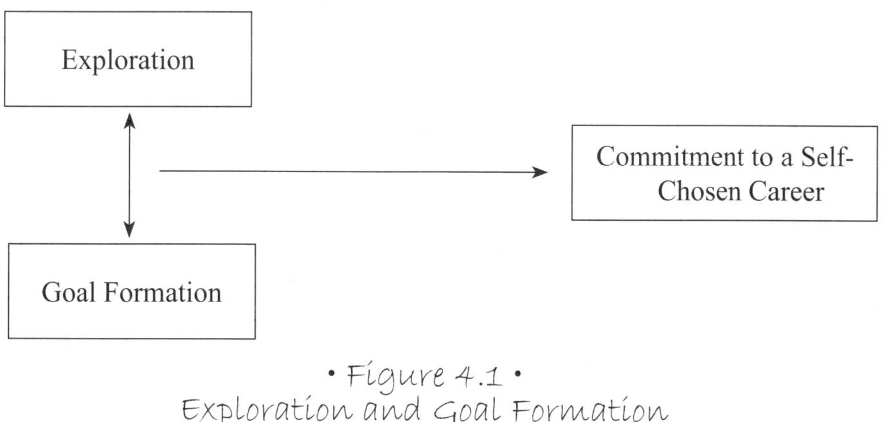

• Figure 4.1 •
Exploration and Goal Formation

Note. From *Identity: Youth and Crisis,* by E. H. Erikson, 1968, New York: Norton. Copyright 1968 by Norton. Adapted with permission.

expresses a focus that means something very important to them, something that they value. To cope with career identity quandaries and opportunities, adolescents frequently employ one of three orientations (Berzonsky, 1996):

1. *Diffused orientation.* Your teen may act in a confused manner, be poorly organized, and be unable to focus on the future. He or she may avoid difficult tasks, career decisions, and opportunities.
2. *Conferred orientation.* Your teen may start to understand his or her place in the world of work not through an autonomous process of exploration and choice but through the eyes of others. He or she may develop career plans that are dominated by the expectations of others.
3. *Information-seeking orientation.* Your teen actively explores and gathers information before making important career decisions. Your teen's commitment to a career direction is an expression of what he or she has found to be intrinsically motivating and personally valuable. We really need to promote this third orientation.

Parents can play a huge role in teaching their children how to develop an information-seeking, exploratory orientation. Studies have found that parents who engage their children in explorations of creative, technical, and cultural activities in childhood have adolescents who use more positive exploratory behaviors during their teenage years (Schmitt-Rodermund & Vondracek, 1999; Vondracek, 1993). These exploratory, information-seeking adolescents have been found to make much better career decisions in high school, college, and young adulthood. Exploration is a good way to counteract the insidious narrowing of your children's hopes and dreams that certain cultural forces attempt to impose on them (like gender roles and racial stereotypes).

Goal Formation

Goals help your children to enhance their achievements in the present and give them the motivation to keep working toward dreams that will come about in the distant future (like becoming a doctor, a business owner, an interior designer, or a research scientist—whatever they one day hope to be). Goals are an expression of one of our most important human assets, planning. Goals expose forethought, the premeditation your children use to approach both the present and future. When you ask your teenagers to fantasize about the career they would like to one day enter, the future life they would like to have, the educational and career aspirations they dream of, and the decisions they are close to making a commitment to, your teenagers are telling you about the goals they are using to imagine a future end state (an ideal place where they want to be someday).

Goals enable us to regulate our actions, invest our energies, and deploy our resources. Goals add a level of organization, coherence, and stability that will increase your children's life satisfaction in adulthood. In adolescence, involvement in career planning activities has been found to help students feel more engaged in their high school (Kenny, Blustein, Haase, Jackson, & Perry, 2006). These ninth graders reported feeling a greater sense of belonging and valuing in their high schools. Adolescents who are able to organize their high school studies around a career goal that means something to them make more successful transitions in young adulthood into the roles of worker and learner, and they report greater levels of satisfaction with their lives 3 years after leaving high school (Lapan et al., 2007).

Now ask yourself, What are the characteristics that distinguish more effective from less effective goals? Box 4.2 lists the Top 10 features of more effective goals. When you are listening to your teenagers describing their goals, check to see whether what they are talking about matches this list. Many studies have found that an effective goal is one that your child has become solidly committed to and expresses something that holds intrinsic worth for them (e.g., Cantor & Sanderson, 1999). Effective goals are self-selected after young people have actively explored their options. Your teenagers should be able to be clear and specific about what their plans are. These plans should represent objectives that

• Box 4.2 •

Top 10 Characteristics of Effective Career Goals

Career goals that promote well-being, life satisfaction, and progress toward a desired future will be more likely to have the following features:

1. Be firmly held, committed to, and consistently pursued
2. Be intrinsically valued
3. Be autonomously chosen as a result of engagement in a substantive process of exploration
4. Be clear and specific
5. Be both challenging and attainable
6. Be closely connected to key decision points
7. Be related to specific behaviors that can be brought under voluntary control
8. Be realistic to one's daily life contexts
9. Be sustained by regular support from one's social contexts
10. Be supported by available personal, social, and tangible resources

are difficult to reach but doable. Easy to reach goals are not valued, and children and adults give up in the face of obstacles they perceive to be impossible to overcome (Locke & Latham, 1990).

At those key moments when decisions have to be made, it should be clear how your teenagers' actions will be influenced by their forward-looking career goals. These goals should be able to show your teens the specific actions that they can control to bring about what they want. These goals lay out a course of action that can be realistically pursued in everyday social contexts at home, at school, and in the community. For example, your child may want to be a marine biologist but not want to move out of the midwestern United States. This goal, although not completely impossible, certainly presents some challenges. Finally, to be effective, your teenagers' goals need to receive your emotional support and whatever resources are required. This is where family, school, and communities can provide a network of unbreakable support to lift all of our children toward valued futures.

Time Is on Your Side

Most adolescents view time as something that extends forever in front of them. It is an unlimited resource that they can burn without worrying that it will ever run out. This understanding of time aides and abets many adolescents to see themselves as indestructible, part of an inevitable force that proceeds in an uninhibited manner toward an open-ended future. In contrast, adults come to the realization that time is really a very precious and limited commodity. It is a gift that is all too soon taken from us. These differing perspectives on time have been found to significantly influence the types of goals that adolescents strive for versus the goals that most adults tend to seek.

Researchers have found that when people (of practically any age) see time as open ended and expansive they choose goals of exploration (Carstensen, Isaacowitz, & Charles, 1999). Adolescents are the prime example. They seem driven to explore and seek information. They are learning about the world around them, how and where they fit in. In contrast, adults are more likely to truly realize that time is finite and limited. In coping with the full realization of this, adults choose goals that establish deeper bonds, connections, and intimacy with others. Adolescent relationships are like the circles a flat stone makes as it skims across the surface of a pond. They are small moments of intense feeling that leap quickly toward the next encounter. Beautiful and mesmerizing, they lightly touch the surface of what is possible in more adult exchanges.

Conclusion

Now is the best time to talk to your adolescents about their career development. Your teenagers feel the pull of time drawing them toward an expansive and unknown future. You can be of great assistance in supporting them to deeply engage in educational and career explorations. Out of these information-seeking activities, effective career goals can be established. Exploration and goal formation can lead your adolescents to find and then commit themselves to a possible future that is intrinsically meaningful and interesting to them. They will then have embraced and greatly benefited from the career identity opportunities of adolescence.

• Target 4 •
Help Your Teenagers Know Themselves

This target emphasizes the need for your teenagers to better understand themselves and the world of work they will soon enter. Better educational and career choices come when young people make decisions by connecting accurate knowledge of self with up-to-date knowledge of the world of work (Pope, 2000). This section focuses on helping you to better understand your teenagers' work values, personality, abilities, talents, and skills. An overview of John Holland's six personality types is provided, which have been extensively studied in relation to occupational entry, career satisfaction, and success in the workplace.

Understand Yourself

Your teenagers' chances of finding a career direction that adds meaning and purpose to their lives will be significantly improved if they act with greater self-understanding and awareness. From the time of Socrates the need to "know thyself" has been an important ingredient for a well-lived life. Nowhere is this truer that in your son's or daughter's career decision making.

Career planning and decision making are enormously enhanced when individuals better understand their work values, personality, preferred working conditions, and abilities. Positive beliefs and identity development need to take root in career directions that are a good match between the unique combination of talents, traits, and values central to the well-being of your child and work environments that actually require the use of these personal preferences. Job satisfaction and performance are enhanced when a more optimal match can be made between what is important to your child and what is demanded in different work settings. However, this kind of self-analysis may be the weakest part of your teenager's preparation to make important educational and career decisions. You may find that this is something your child really has not given much thought to—a very good reason for you to dig deep into this target.

Adolescents need to begin a systematic exploration that will eventually lead to the creation of a more optimal match between what is most important to them and those career pathways that are more likely to encourage (if not demand) the expression of these personal preferences. Your teenagers need to understand what work values are important to them; what parts of their personality they should seek to express in a career choice; what working conditions (working indoors vs. outdoors, or the length of training) they would prefer; and what abilities, talents, and skills they would want to utilize in a career.

Your teenagers are moving into a developmental stage in which it is important for them to better understand themselves. In my experience, most teenagers have not given this a great deal of thought. If you were to just ask them about their work values, they would likely stare back at you with an "I'm out of here" expression. Think of this as new territory for your teenagers. They will like discussing this with you but will need a little background knowledge to see what you are getting at. This chapter gives you that information, packaged to help you orient your teenagers to these critical lifelong issues.

Work Values. Your children will be more content and satisfied in a career that rewards them for pursuing values that provide direction to their work lives. As your teenagers begin to seriously consider what career paths they might choose to follow, they will make judgments about how well this direction "sits" with them. What they are doing is comparing each possible career path to an internal code. When it seems likely that a career direction will allow your teenagers to act in certain preferred ways or achieve what they think is desirable, this career path moves up on the list of occupations more likely to really be considered.

The values your teenagers use to assess whether or not a career is a good match for them is one of the yardsticks they will use to rank order career options. Right now, they most likely use a "default" set of criteria about which they have not really given much thought. For example, their decision making may be dominated by a desire to enter a career that the important people in their lives (like you) would find to be prestigious. Your teenagers may not even be aware that their need to enter a prestigious career (however they may understand or misconstrue prestigious careers to be) may act as a jail keeper that locks up a range of good options in a "not to be considered" category. In addition, your teenagers may have already identified critical values that they want in a career. Your teens will cling to these perspectives as they gird themselves to meet the many unknowns that they sense are just ahead of them.

What can you do about this? First, before you have this discussion with your teenager, let's think about work values together. Box 4.3 lists 21 work values and preferred working conditions that people often identify as being important to them. Think about these work values and conditions and how they apply to your own life. Then you will be better able to introduce this idea to your teenagers by showing them how this fits for you. You will use this information when we do a work values exercise in Chapter 7.

Personality. If your children can express the parts of their personality that are important to their sense of being and identity in the world in their work, they will be both more satisfied and more

• Box 4.3 •

Work Values and Preferred Working Conditions

1. Earning a high income
2. Having an opportunity to be creative
3. Helping others
4. Earning recognition or prestige in your career
5. Being able to work independently
6. Being a leader and making decisions
7. Having flexibility in your work hours
8. Having a variety of work tasks to do
9. Being curious and solving problems
10. Working indoors or outdoors
11. Using your hands and doing physical things in your work
12. Being your own boss
13. Achieving economic security
14. Working with specific tools, technologies, animals, plants, people, or ideas
15. Entering a career that requires a long training time after high school (like a 4-year college degree, MBA, PhD, or MD)
16. Entering a career that requires a relatively shorter training time after high school (like a 2-year associate's degree, specialized training, and/or certification program)
17. Working in an organization as part of a work team
18. Earning advancements in one's career
19. Taking risks and being adventurous either physically (such as in a special services unit in the armed forces) or in the intellectual problems or economic ventures that you pursue
20. Having the autonomy to exercise some personal control over the work tasks and problems that are the focus of your energies
21. Being compatible with your religious orientation

productive in their careers. John Holland's (1997) seminal research and thinking in this area have highlighted how career choice represents an active search process in which individuals try to locate a career path that will allow and encourage them to express important personality traits in their work. He and his colleagues distilled this down to six personality types and then categorized all work environments according to which combination of these six personality types were required. Box 4.4 explains each of these six personality types.

One way to understand the idea of fit between individuals and their work environment is to think of the old expression "birds of a feather flock together and flocks are different from each other." For a long time we have known that, on average, people who work in a particular career tend to have more in common than people who work in markedly different work environments. For example, both school counselors and social workers share a strong Social orientation to help others (promoting individual growth and development). The variety of different work environments that are employment options for counselors and social workers are tied together by this Social theme (whether they are employed in child protective custody services or in public schools). It is not only expressed in the preferred personality style of the workers. It is also embodied in the mandatory daily, weekly, and monthly job tasks, duties, and requirements. In contrast, although the social scientists with whom I work at my university are concerned with helping others, they really want to

• Box 4.4 •

Holland's Personality Types

Personality Type	*Description*
Realistic	These individuals like hands-on mechanical activities and tasks that are well ordered and often occur outdoors. Such people are often quite mechanically skilled and prefer working with tools, machines, and animals. They are likely to be employed in jobs such as air traffic controllers, engineers, and military officers.
Investigative	These individuals are likely to be curious about how and why things work; they are analytical and scientific. They tend not to like jobs in sales, a lot of social interaction, or work tasks that require overly repetitive activities. They are more likely to be employed in jobs such as chemists, computer systems analysts, and physicians.
Artistic	These individuals like tasks that require the creation of new forms of expression. They prefer using their imagination to grapple with ambiguous problems. These people work in areas such as creative writing, illustration, and law.
Social	These individuals enjoy working with people in helping, training, and teaching work situations. They tend not to like working with tools or their hands. They are likely to be employed in jobs such as social workers, teachers, and nurses.
Enterprising	These individuals like sales and leadership roles where they can make a profit economically and further the goals of their organization. They tend to be employed in jobs such as sales representatives, chief executive officers, and life insurance agents.
Conventional	These individuals like to perform well-ordered tasks within a clearly defined organizational hierarchy. They may prefer work tasks such as data manipulation and record keeping. They are more likely to be employed in jobs such as bank tellers, accountants, and nursing home administrators.

investigate particular aspects of the human condition in an analytical, rigorous, and scientific manner (Investigative type). They do not want to have a large client or student caseload that requires them to spend large chunks of their day providing direct services to individuals.

What do you think your Holland personality type is? What about your children? You will learn more about this when you do a personality assessment exercise with your teenager in Chapter 7.

Abilities, Talents, and Skills. Of all the issues that we will talk about, this is the most difficult and troubling topic for me. You see, I was not a good high school student. My focus was on basketball, soccer, and girls (not necessarily in that order). I know firsthand what it is like to score low on a test like the SAT and be told by a school counselor that I wouldn't be accepted at a 4-year college. Because of the consistent support from my parents, I did go to a 4-year college. There I learned an interesting thing: If you actually read the assignments, your grades go up. I didn't become a good student until my junior year in college because I didn't know how to learn. I was missing a lot of needed skills.

When I got the crazy idea to go to graduate school, I knew I would again have to run the gauntlet of standardized entrance examinations. However, this time I got smart. I signed up with one of the national test-taking preparation services that are now so widely available. Admittedly, I took this very seriously and did all of the classes and practice tests that were available. It finally dawned on me how to do those analogy problems and the basics of high school math (which I had been physically but not mentally present for as a teenager). I had already been working very successfully in the human services field with very difficult adolescents, and my scores on the Graduate Record Examination were good enough for me to be accepted into several PhD programs. In the application process, it was clear that although the work experience was nice, what really counted were the test scores. Thankfully this situation is beginning to change.

Your teenagers will enter a world that in some ways has gone test crazy. In recent years, some of the better colleges have moved to de-emphasize (if not get rid of) standardized tests in favor of a more holistic understanding of the applicant (one of the reasons why your teenager's personal statement on college applications has to be very well done). However, parents need a way to talk to their teenagers about their abilities, talents, and skills that will protect them from the gross misuse of tests that is quite possible in a culture that has come to so embrace them. Now, don't get me wrong. I respect and honor good testing and the accurate interpretation of test results. It is just that the leading tests today do not measure the critical range of motivational factors that could ignite children's imagination and empower their potential. You need to be able to speak to your teenagers about their strengths and possible weaknesses in ways that do not limit possible career futures.

It is very clear to me that each of my three daughters has a very distinctive pattern of abilities, talents, and skills. The oldest is great at remembering and following directions. She is very accurate and detail oriented in her work. She approaches tasks in a bottom-up fashion, linking bits of information together to solve problems. My middle daughter fixes our computer. She sees the big picture and integrates bits of information into her more general theories. The youngest daughter can combine visual images and words in humorous, insightful, and highly creative ways. Just don't ask her what time of the day it is or what month or season comes next.

What is most important is that each of my daughters is interacting with the world in increasingly more complex and sophisticated ways. They are really using their potential in the daily tasks and trials that school requires of them. In mastering these challenges, they are becoming self-regulated learners. This internally motivated approach to the world frees them to use all of their abilities, talents, and skills to their utmost potential. Soon, we will focus our attention on helping your teenagers become self-regulated, lifelong learners. In Chapter 7 you will do an exercise with your teenagers in which you explore their abilities without closing doors to future dreams.

Understanding the World of Work

In the 21st century, the workplace your teenagers will enter is not one that your parents would recognize. Long gone are the once secure, high-paying manufacturing jobs that required little formal education or training. The supersonic pace of technological innovation and globalization has transformed every aspect of our work lives.

The new economic opportunity structure is creating a diverse array of technology-related high-wage, high-skill careers. However, these jobs are only available to individuals who have mastered rigorous academic programs of study, some of which can be completed in 2 years or less (following graduation from high school). In my state, a local technical community college has created an integrated manufacturing technology training program. This program trains students in electronics, robotics, computer-assisted machining, and quality control processes. Students receive a comprehensive curriculum that integrates training in machining, electrical motors, and microcomputers with critical thinking, mathematics, and interpersonal communication skill development. Training on the latest equipment available in the workplace, students seamlessly transition into careers such as electronics technician, automation technician, machining technician, computer numerical control programmer, industrial maintenance technician, and manufacturing technician.

Students can graduate from this training program with a 2-year associate of science degree or shorter certificate of completion. In addition, a new laser photonics program is being planned. For more information about these and other training programs available at this technical community college go to www.linnstate.edu. There are technical community colleges around the country and near you that are developing training programs such as this. In Chapter 7 you and your teenagers will learn how to gather vital, accurate, and up-to-date information (such as salary, demand for the job, and required training) about careers in the 21st century.

Conclusion

Self-understanding is a critical component of making a more informed educational and career decision. In Chapter 7 you and your teenager will do a number of exercises together in which you both will learn more about yourself and each other as well as learn about available educational and career opportunities. Fitting this understanding of self to knowledge of the work world will greatly assist your teen to choose wisely. And with the current cost of college tuition, I can think of thousands of reasons why this is a good idea.

• Target 5 •
Help Your Teenagers Pursue Their Interests

Adolescence is a key time to expose young people to new learning situations that will broaden the range of educational and career activities that they are interested in pursuing. Interest patterns begin to stabilize in our mid-20s and can then be very resistant to change. Most young people have not had the kinds of learning experiences that will help them to know whether or not a particular career path would be of interest to them. In the absence of better information, they are at risk of making faulty decisions based on the limiting influence of factors such as gender-role stereotypes. We need to help our teenagers experience a wide array of educational and career situations to help them expand their choices. Finding a career that your teenagers really like and want to get up in the morning and go to work to will add satisfaction and well-being to their lives.

Interests Are Important

When your teenagers tell you what they really like to do, pay very close attention. If you want to know what career paths your teenagers are most likely to pursue, talk to them about their interests. Actions follow from the pattern of interests that begin to show themselves during the adolescent years. Tests that measure career interests have been found to be very predictive of the kinds of occupations young people enter 4, 8, and 12 years down the road (Harmon, Hansen, Borgen, & Hammer, 1994). A longitudinal study of gifted college students found that scores on an interest inventory taken 10 years earlier did a very good job of predicting the college major these talented young people were now pursuing (Achter, Lubinski, Benbow, & Eftekhari-Sanjani, 1999). Another study at an elite, east coast college for women found that if these very bright young women did not enter their freshman year with an already developed interest in mathematics it was extremely unlikely (regardless of their math ability levels) that they would choose mathematics as their college major (Civian & Schley, 1996). In many cases, interests trump abilities in determining a career direction that will bring meaning, purpose, and fulfillment to your child's life.

We know a lot about vocational interests. For example, we know that people who work in similar careers share a common set of interests that make them very different from workers in other occupations. Think about the Holland types we discussed earlier. Women who are geologists like to engage in scientific and analytical activities (Investigative), mechanical and outdoors activities (Realistic), and use their imagination to deal with ambiguous tasks (Artistic) much more than women employed in different kinds of careers. Women who are successfully and satisfactorily employed as bankers enjoy working on well-ordered tasks within a stable organization (Conventional) and engaging in sales and leadership activities (Enterprising) much more so than do women in general (and women who work as geologists). Men who are satisfactorily employed as marketing executives like sales and leadership activities (Enterprising) and using their imagination to solve ambiguous problems (Artistic). Men working as computer programmers/systems analysts like analytical tasks that require them to be curious (Investigative), use their imagination to solve ambiguous problems (Artistic), and work with machines and technology (Realistic) (Harmon et al., 1994).

Interest patterns tend to stabilize around age 25. However, there can be a great deal of change in interests across our working lives depending on the learning experiences and opportunities that we pursue. For example, after taking and successfully mastering several statistics classes in my doctoral program, I developed a strong interest in data analysis. This was one of the determining factors in leading me to seek a faculty position at a research university where I could blend this newly developing interest with long-standing preferences (my interest in learning more about human development and history).

In the absence of such major life-altering encounters that motivate us to develop new parts of ourselves, interests can be quite resistant to change. Several studies have found that even after experiencing severe spinal cord injuries that can lead to quadriplegia and paraplegia, the interest patterns of these individuals are not different from what they were before their accidents (Rohe & Krause, 1998). The interest patterns of individuals experiencing severe spinal cord injuries were found to be just as stable as the interest patterns of a nondisabled comparison group. In addition, workers in the same occupations but living and working in different countries have interest patterns that are more similar to each other than to people who live in the same country but work in different occupations (Fouad & Hansen, 1987). Interest patterns have been found to be a very useful tool to assist individuals from different ethnic, cultural, and racial backgrounds with their career and life planning decisions.

Where Do Interests Come From?

Interests are developed from the interaction between the person and the environment. At least 33% of the variability in your teenagers' career interest patterns is likely due to their unique genetic makeup. Twin studies in behavioral genetics have found that many of the things that we are concerned with in career development have a substantial genetic component (e.g., personality, work values, job satisfaction, and vocational and recreational interests). An additional 11% of the variability in interest patterns can be explained by shared environmental factors that family members have in common. This leaves about 56% that is explained by experiences unique to the individual and the error currently residing in our measurement instruments. It is the interaction between the genetic makeup of your children and the environmental opportunities available to them that increases or decreases the likelihood that certain interests and talents will come to the fore and be expressed in their eventual career decisions (Betsworth et al., 1994).

The ability of underlying genetic predispositions to shape interests in different occupations varies a great deal across careers. For example, it seems that interest in business-related activities is largely due to environmental experiences unique to the individual: 65% of the variance in one's interest in merchandising is due to unique experiences that the individual has had (as well as 71% of the interest in sales activities and 68% of the interest in business management activities; Betsworth et al., 1994). It may be that the interest to become an entrepreneur truly depends upon learning environments that either nourish the creation of such dreams or let them die on the vine.

The learning environments that nurture your children (home, school, and community) provide the foundation for the development of positive self-efficacy expectations. The self-efficacy beliefs that your children come to hold about their competence to successfully perform tasks evolve from their interaction with the world around them. When your teenagers master an important life challenge (like solving a difficult geometry problem that has been assigned for homework) or observe important role models solving real-world work-related problems (like listening to you talk about how you successfully handled an important meeting at work), they are gathering information about themselves that can be used to construct more adaptive and successful expectations about their own capabilities. These perceptions of their abilities have been found to be a major determinant of career interests. A key to helping your teenagers develop a wide range of vocational interests is to provide opportunities in which they can learn what is possible either by performing a task in a competent manner or by watching others manage difficult career challenges.

Gifted Children

Much has been written about the special needs of gifted children. These are children who seem to possess aptitudes for different learning tasks that are well above the norms expected of their peers. Interest patterns can show you some of the potentially debilitating challenges confronting gifted teenagers, as well as the exciting opportunities that could come about in their future. For example, significant problems can arise when you have talents that cut across career domains that are markedly different from each other. In this case, your teenagers may become interested in divergent activities that are not easily found together in a single occupation.

What if your child has exceptional talent in the areas of working with technology and in the performing arts? They may love to spend large chunks of time by themselves working on intricate solutions to computer programming problems, but they also may really look forward to interacting with others as on-air interviewers and personalities for their high school radio station. Now what do they do?

One of the significant challenges faced by gifted teenagers is how to find a direction that enables them to integrate their divergent talents and interests into a single career. What jobs would allow these young people to do both computer programming and creative/applied art activities? It can be very difficult and frustrating for these students to integrate their multiple talents and interests into a single focus that leads to a college major and career. It can also be an exciting adventure to engage with your teenagers in this career exploration process (Shoffner & Newsome, 2001). The activities provided in Chapters 6 and 7 will help you to make this journey.

Conclusion

It takes time and the support of loving parents to help young people find creative ways to infuse their interests into a lifestyle that brings them joy and self-fulfillment. It could be that certain interests become hobbies and lead to the rejuvenating rewards of treasured leisure activities. You can best help your teenagers by talking to them about their interests. The exercises in Chapter 7 are designed to help you help your talented teenagers do exactly this. Adolescence is a great time to expand horizons and explore new vistas. In helping your teenagers to do this, you will give them the best chance to discover new interests and broaden their life choices.

• Target 6 •
Help Your Teenagers Learn How to Learn

Achievement equals choice. Academic achievement is now the required passport for entry into an exciting and wildly diverse range of high-skill, high-wage careers. Unless you have other means of securing your children's future, they will only be able to get the opportunities that they really want if they develop into the kind of lifelong learner that the economy of the 21st century rewards. This foundation has to be laid during the prekindergarten through high school years. This target will help you to better understand what successful self-regulated learners do to enhance their academic achievement (Lapan, Kardash, & Turner, 2002; Zimmerman, 2000). In addition, strategies are outlined for how your family, your child's school, and your community can help your teenager to become a successful lifelong learner.

Early Achievement Matters

National data show without any doubt that those young people who become more effective learners and pass more rigorous courses in high school go to college and do better in their careers. For example, within 2 years of graduating from high school, 83% of the young people who had taken and passed algebra and geometry were in college. However, only 36% of the young people who did not take and pass algebra and geometry were in college. If a young person from a low-income family takes and passes algebra and geometry, he or she is 3 times more likely to enter college than someone from a low-income family who did not have this preparation in high school. Young people with better standardized math achievement test scores earn, on average, 38% more per hour and are much less likely to be unemployed (U.S. Department of Education, 1997).

Your involvement is key to getting your teenagers to take and pass more rigorous coursework in high school. For example, 48% of a nationwide sample of high school students in the United States who said that their parents regularly spoke to them about their plans for what high school classes they would take actually took geometry by the end of their sophomore year in high school (U.S. Department of Education, 1997). Taking and passing rigorous courses in high school requires your teenagers to be more fully engaged in their academic work. If they develop a more self-directed investment and commitment to their studies, they will achieve more and create the attitudes and skills needed to be more successful lifelong learners.

What Is a Self-Regulated Learner, and Why Is It Important to Be One?

More successful students act in distinctive ways. They are very purposeful and creative in how they approach school assignments and tests. By employing highly effective learning strategies, they improve their academic performance and get the most out of their abilities. They are more fully engaged in classroom activities. The success and satisfaction that these young people experience in relation to their academic work forge a pattern that makes future successes and satisfactions much more likely. More successful learners exert some degree of control over the planning, performance, and outcome phases of academic learning events (Zimmerman, 2000).

More Successful Learners Plan Ahead. Before completing an important school project or writing a paper or taking a test, more successful learners think ahead about the task and how they will handle it. They do not impulsively jump in. Instead, they may try to break the project down into its important components (do a task analysis). They think of themselves in very confident and positive terms, envisioning themselves completing a high-quality product. They expect their performance to be top notch and set challenging goals and standards. More successful learners are often more concerned about mastering a task and improving their knowledge and skills. They do not get bogged down competing with or comparing themselves to others. They are focused on doing their best.

More Successful Learners Watch How They Are Doing and Make Changes That Improve Their Performance. When performing an academic task, self-regulated learners use highly effective strategies to monitor how they are doing and make adjustments as they are needed. They know when they don't know something and then act to do something about it before their performance is negatively affected. Box 4.5 lists seven learning strategies that enhance academic performance. More effective learners not only use strategies like these, but they also observe how they are doing and use this feedback to improve what they are doing as they are doing it.

• Box 4.5 •

Effective Learning Strategies Used by More Successful Students

Strategy	*Description*
Identifying important information	Separate essential from nonessential information by using "signaling devices" in the text such as underlining and highlighting words or phrases (Mandler, 1984).
Summarizing important information	Identify main ideas that can be used to organize details and more specific information (Ormrod, 1999).
Using prior knowledge	Connect new information to what is already known and has previously been learned (Gagne, Yekovich, & Yekovich, 1993).
Notetaking	Record the main ideas and the details that support these ideas (Ormrod, 1999).
Organizing information	Connect information that has to be learned in ways that show the important relationships between the different pieces of the information, such as creating an outline of the major topics, developing a graph of the content that has to be remembered, or constructing a concept map that shows the relationship between important ideas (Gagne et al., 1993).
Monitoring comprehension	Stop to ask themselves whether or not they truly understand what they are reading or learning. If the answer is no, they do something right away to fix the problem (Baker, 1989).
Using imagery	Construct images to represent the meaning in a text. Mnemonic imagery is really helpful to learn lists, pairs of words, and facts (Ormrod, 1999). For example, most counselors remember Holland's six personality types by using the mnemonic aid "RIASEC." See if you can recall Holland's model using the RIASEC strategy.

More Successful Learners Think About How They Did and What They Could Do to Improve in the Future. After finishing a project, self-regulated learners reflect on what has happened and how they have done. If things have not gone well for them, they tend to attribute the reasons to external factors that they have some control over. (They might say something like "I didn't really try very hard, but next time I will do my best.") They do not understand their failure to be due to things that they can't control. (They are less likely to say something like "I am not good at math, never have been, never will be.") The information gained from their self-reflections will be connected to the questions they ask themselves during the planning phases of future learning events. Thus they create a self-enhancing, self-fulfilling cycle that both reinforces and motivates better academic performance. The use of these self-regulating behaviors leads to high levels of performance and persistence that are more regularly demonstrated by successful students. This stands in sharp contrast to the self-doubt and avoidance of academic tasks that are more often seen in academic nonachievers.

How Can Your Teenagers Become More Effective Self-Regulated Learners?

This question is surprisingly easy to answer but difficult to do something about. It comes down to shaping and changing the behavior of the adults with whom your teenagers interact. The major environments in which your children live (home, school, and community) will either increase their chances of becoming more self-regulated learners or make this a very unlikely prospect. The adults within these primary settings create opportunities for your children to take initiative, have some responsibility, make some decisions on their own, and learn how to live well with others. These critical learning environments can go a long way toward assisting young people in experiencing mastery in some activity and a sense that they belong in positive ways with others. The hardest part may be getting the adults in each setting to change some of their behaviors. When adults are more strategic in their actions and work together in a cohesive fashion, the learning behaviors of children become much more malleable and open to influence. Here is what needs to happen for your teenagers when they are at home, in school, or out in the community.

Five Things You Should Do at Home

1. Stay actively involved in your children's learning. Just because your teenagers have entered high school does not mean that you should now back out of the picture, figuring you have done all you can do. As your teenagers transition from middle school to junior high and then to high school, the road will get more difficult. Rigorous classes make greater demands on their time. Hours spent on homework will greatly increase.

   This is a very difficult time for parents. The content of what my children are expected to learn in difficult courses leaves me in the dust. I may not know the chemistry, biology, Latin, Spanish, or precalculus that they are learning. You may take one look at their books and be swept over with unpleasant memories of when you had to take these same subjects in high school (or avoided taking them).

   So, how can we be of any help to them? We support them by staying emotionally involved and connected. You may not know the answers to difficult homework questions, but by working together you can find additional help when needed. For example, we routinely get e-mail progress updates from teachers. Homework assignments can be found online. You can easily contact most teachers. The vast percentage of teachers will meet with students either before or after school to provide extra help. But you and your teenagers need to initiate this. As the parent, you need to make sure that your children get this extra help. Whether your teenagers are struggling to pass or are getting top grades in the course, every student can benefit from this individualized attention.
2. Be an authoritative parent. Your teenager needs you to enforce rules and standards while at the same time you encourage open communication, independence, and autonomy. Parents who are too permissive do not provide the structure their teenagers need. Parents who are too authoritarian do not provide the opportunities for their teenagers to exercise some control over their lives. It is a balancing act to be sure.

   Your teenager is neither adult nor child. It is a very complex parenting skill to impose structure while at the same time providing room for adolescents to express their autonomy. Your teenagers need you to be both strong and empathic at the same time. Keep the lines of communication open. Think of it this way, some research is now suggesting that the prefrontal cortex doesn't stop growing until people are in their early 20s. Because of this, the ability of adolescents to be reflective in their judgments, organize tasks (take a look at their rooms if you can stand the shock), and regulate intense emotions has not yet fully matured. For both boys and girls, the onset of puberty increases testosterone levels that then swell their amygdala (an almond-shaped mass of gray matter associated with, among other things, feelings of fear and aggression). This intensifies teenagers' irritability, fears, and anger. As you parent, you have to stay in the game and ride out the storm. Your teenagers need both space and structure, all at the same time.
3. Create an effective learning environment for your children at home. Pay attention to how you can shape both the way time is spent after school, evenings, and weekends and the physical space where your teenagers study. I am not suggesting that you become a prison

warden in your own home, but you need to pay attention to the routines that dictate how your teenagers spend time after school. When will they study? Where will they study? By the time your children reach high school, much of this should already be internalized and self-directed by them, an outcome of the routines that you consistently put in place during the elementary school years. If it is not, you will need to be very directive about this.

It is not too late. Work out a contract with them. Build in positive reinforcements (e.g., record favorite shows so they can watch them after their homework is done). Don't let your kids isolate themselves in their rooms or on the Internet or with their electronic games. You pay the bills; video games are a luxury you finance.

Engage them—this is worth fighting for. You need to be serious and let your teenagers know that this is their job right now and that they must put forth their best efforts. Focus on the effort and not the outcome. When your teenagers are working hard, commend them for that. Developing good work habits will pay off in the long run. Don't fixate on the grades.

4. Help your children to believe in themselves. Your beliefs and expectations will have a lot to do with how your children feel about themselves as learners. As we discussed earlier, if you hold traditional gender-role attitudes such as math is harder for girls than boys, you may unwittingly undercut your daughter's self-confidence to do higher level math. This may make your teenagers more vulnerable to misinterpreting information about their competence. On average, math grades go down as the courses become more difficult. So what if your son or daughter got a B⁺ in 9th-grade algebra, a B⁻ in 10th-grade geometry, and a C⁺ in 11th-grade trigonometry? Should they take precalculus in their senior year? If they have doubts about themselves, they may just see their declining grades as a statement of their lack of ability and not want to risk getting a C. They may miss entirely the normative pattern that most students' grades decline as you proceed through this sequence.
5. Provide a safe, structured, and drug-free home. Have fun with your teenagers; do activities together that you all enjoy. But be honest with yourself: Are you providing a home environment that encourages your teenagers to avoid using illegal substances? You have to be there and be involved to make sure this is not happening. Know where your teenagers are and how they are spending their time. To get your teenagers through these tough years, you need to be there for them. Be savvy and vigilant.

Five Things Your Teenager's School Should Do

1. Engage your teenagers in a quality curriculum. Easy courses that let your teenagers slide by will not get it done in today's world. The school should deluge your teenagers with tough, rigorous, high-quality courses. An effort should be made to make at least some of these courses interesting to your teens. The more class work can be connected to real-world contexts, the more interested and motivated your teenagers will be in their studies. If your teenagers can see the relevance in what they are learning to possible desired career futures, this will be a great advantage to them.

   An important part of a quality curriculum is the teaching practices that are routinely used for instruction. Are your children being taught with methods that encourage them to focus on improving their skills and deepening their understanding? Or is there an overemphasis on competing against others? Children who are taught with methods that focus on mastery score higher on tests of cognitive ability and academic achievement. An overemphasis on performance and outdoing others can lead teenagers to experience feelings of inferiority to others and looking bad in front of their peers. As a result, they may be less willing to take risks and learn new things. This is not the self-confidence of a self-regulated, successful lifelong learner that we are trying to promote.
2. Help your children to have good relationships. If I could give my children one thing as a resilience factor to cope with school, I would want them to have a good, caring, and con-

nected set of relationships with their teachers. One of the leading educational researchers in the United States went so far as to call this the fourth "R" in education (Reading, Riting, Rithmatic, and Relationships; Ladd, 1999). Kids who have better relationships with teachers, peers, and authority figures do better in school. School is a place where they feel they belong, feel safe, and want to attend.

3. Be enriched by diversity. Your children are going to live in a pluralistic democracy that must compete in a global marketplace. This is a very real centerpiece of their future. Isolating them to homogenous learning experiences will not prepare them for this reality. Information has no geographic borders. As part of its mission, the school should help your children to know about, be respectful of, accept, and be enriched by diversity. They will work with people from every corner of this earth. Success will more likely flow to the individual who can create more effective relationships in the face of this enormous and life-enriching diversity of cultures, races, and religions.
4. Home/school connection. When I was growing up, it was pretty clear to me that the school I attended and the home I lived in were on the same page. Each reinforced the values of the other. I could not drive a wedge between them. Your children's school needs to be open to creating this working alliance with you. Teachers, counselors, principals, and parents working together can be an impenetrable wall that keeps teenagers thriving ahead to master new academic challenges. Everyone should have the same goal, helping children maximize their talents and become satisfied, happy, and productive young adults.
5. Utilize school counselors. Counselors can be a great source of help for your children. The American School Counselor Association directs professional school counselors to promote the academic, social/emotional, and career development of every child in a school (see for yourself at www.schoolcounselor.org). Your children's school counselor should be actively engaged in helping students to select and succeed in rigorous classes. They should provide career exploration and post–high school planning services. They are there for informal, short-term counseling and for referral to private counseling if your teenager needs additional help. The counselors who are now getting their graduate school training are not the same as the counselors you may have had when you were in school. A major revolution in the field is occurring; take advantage of it. Don't get trapped in negative stereotypes you may hold because of the counselor in your school who may not have helped you (Gysbers & Henderson, 2006).

Five Things Your Community Should Do

1. Provide many structured experiences for your teenagers to choose from. Girl Scouts, Boy Scouts, youth sports, theater groups for young people, biology clubs, outward-bound experiences—the list is endless. Your teenagers need the chance to engage with peers and adults in activities that they find intrinsically interesting. These experiences should be organized, include positive adult role models, provide support, and be freely chosen by your teenagers. Within these interactions, your teenagers can learn how to create meaning, direction, and order in their lives (especially when it comes to making important decisions). After school, weekend, and summer activities energize your teenagers and engage them in vibrant interaction with others. Sitting at home alone in front of the tube, computer, or latest video game is not a recipe for success.
2. Safe and drug free. Don't kid yourself; your teenagers have relatively easy access to illegal drugs. They are likely to know classmates who sometimes come to school high. They know kids who take pills from their parents and siblings. They know peers who sneak alcohol from their parents and sometimes may even drink with their parents. Each of the environments within which your teenagers live must provide them a safe haven if they are to develop their abilities to the fullest extent possible.

3. Community, school, and home partnerships. One thing that we learned from the federal School-to-Work Opportunities Act of 1994 is that businesses, community leaders, parents, and schools can work together effectively to enhance the educational and career development of all young people. High school students who were planning on going to 4-year universities or 2-year technical community colleges eagerly latched onto learning opportunities that gave them some real-world exposure and experience. My niece worked in a pharmacy, with a pharmacist, while studying chemistry in high school. One school person in a rural community in my state told me that he had two young women work with a local medical doctor while they were taking difficult science courses. Both of these students graduated from high school and left to study premedicine at very respected universities. Across the United States, businesses overwhelmingly got on board to create learning opportunities for young people. To do this, they had to overcome some big obstacles, including insurance liability. It would be a great advantage for your teenagers and the young people in your community if a partnership network could be created and maintained.
4. Positive peer groups. Teenagers thrive when they are connected to a group of friends whose lives are heading in a productive direction. One of the worst things that can happen to your children is identifying with and committing themselves to a deviant peer group. This is one of the stepping-stones toward juvenile delinquency and antisocial behavior in adulthood. Engaging your teenagers in structured community activities connects them to peers with like interests and more achievement-oriented approaches to life.
5. Cohesive communities with positive expectations. Leading sociologists have described the plight of many of our communities in the United States where parents find themselves isolated, having to raise children mostly on their own without the support of others. In the small town that I grew up in, if you were acting up in the neighborhood, adults (not just relatives and parents) let you know about it and held you accountable. Unfortunately, too many young people grow up without the benefits of this extended network of adult supervision. Somewhat related to this, some communities hold very low expectations for what they consider possible for their young people. The adults don't really believe that really good economic and career things can happen for youth in their community. These lowered beliefs about future success are then unwittingly communicated to the next generation. The cycle is complete.

Conclusion

It is very possible for your teenagers to become effective, self-regulated, and successful lifelong learners. This is a necessary passport for success in the work world of today and tomorrow. The strategies outlined in this chapter can help improve your teenagers' academic development by linking what happens at home, in school, and out in your community. When we work together in partnership and common cause, we can help all of our children secure meaningful and valued futures.

• Target 7 •
Help Your Teenagers Get Along Better With Others

The very best opportunities in life that await your children will be made possible through the quality of their relationships with others. This is as true in the workplace as it will be in your children's private lives. This target emphasizes the social competencies that young people need if they are to meet success in their careers. Your teenagers will be called upon to exhibit a sophisticated network of relationship skills. These will include social and prosocial skills, diversity skills, responsible work habits, positive personal qualities, balanced emotional states, and the ability to make their own jobs (be an entrepreneur).

Social Competence in the 21st-Century Workplace

Your children can have all the talents in the world, but if they cannot get along with others, their success and satisfaction in both their careers and personal lives will be much less than they could be. Of course, you can find exceptions to this. Individuals with extraordinary technical abilities can find or create a niche in an organization where they will be left alone to do their thing. But, on average, being successful in a career and experiencing a sense of well-being in adulthood are closely tied to our ability to relate to and work well with others. If you get along with your coworkers and supervisors, you will be more productive on your job, experience greater job satisfaction, and be less likely to leave that job (Wanberg & Kammeyer-Mueller, 2000).

Your children will be expected to work collaboratively as part of a team to solve complex problems and complete high-quality projects. The global economy and changing nature of the workplace will reward those who can effectively work with others who may be markedly different from themselves in culture, race, gender, and religious orientation. If your teenagers are socially competent, they will be more likely to thrive in adulthood and assume positions of leadership. As laid out in Box 4.6, to be socially competent in the 21st-century workplace, young people need to develop social skills and prosocial behaviors, diversity skills, a set of responsible work habits, positive personal qualities, a positive personal balance and emotional state, and the ability to become an entrepreneur (if they should so desire).

• Box 4.6 •

Social Competence for the 21st-Century Workplace

Social Skills
- Build and maintain effective relationships
- Communicate, communicate, communicate
- Care for others and the environment
- Develop and use prosocial behaviors

Diversity Skills
- Be knowledgeable of differences
- Be respectful of differences
- Be accepting of differences
- Be enriched by differences

Responsible Work Habits
- Develop a sense of personal industry
- Have a good work ethic
- Show initiative
- Be responsible and dependable

Positive Personal Qualities
- Be a leader in the workplace
- Have self-esteem
- Use good personal hygiene
- Present yourself effectively

Positive Personal Balance and Emotional State
- Don't be anxious
- Don't be depressed
- Don't be shy

Entrepreneurship
- Make your own job

Social Skills

Your teenagers will face many social skill challenges in their pursuit of a personally valued and meaningful career. Success will be more likely if they consistently enact a positive self-presentation style with customers, coworkers, and supervisors. Being able to effectively solve interpersonal conflicts, negotiate, and compromise with others is advantageous. Being able to effectively express themselves in speech and in writing will earn your teenagers big paycheck rewards. Hearing another person's point of view and then taking that into consideration will help to make your teenagers more respected, valued, and successful on the job. Being able to work effectively with others who are immensely different from themselves (in race, religion, ethnicity, or culture) may be a key to your teenagers' and our future economic well-being.

Your teenagers will achieve more if they can ask for help, take guidance from others, and learn from the people around them. Taking direction from authority figures is a stepping-stone to keeping and then beginning to advance in most jobs. In every sector of the economy, socially skilled adults gravitate toward and are nominated by others to assume positions of leadership, decision making, and influence.

Social skills competence is not guaranteed in a young person's life. Many children exhibit glaring social skills deficits that lead them into repetitive patterns of failed social exchanges with both peers and adults. They may not be able to make good friends. They may be too aggressive or too easily angered. They can be too bossy or self-centered, or both. Some children shrink away into the woodwork in their classes or on the playground. They are overly timid, shy, unresponsive in their communication with others, and act in withdrawn and passive ways.

The beliefs that young people use to navigate and interpret their social world can be faulty. For example, boys who are overly aggressive tend to misinterpret the intentions of others. They are more likely to think others will be hostile and aggressive toward them. This consistent pattern of misinterpreting the intentions of others puts these young people at greater risk for repeatedly stumbling into exchanges that are rife for conflict and all-out confrontation.

This lack of social skills development and faulty social beliefs have severe consequences. If your teenagers cannot get along with the other kids in class or with their teachers, they will do much more poorly in those classes and will likely be rejected by peers whose lives are heading in more positive directions. This is a recipe for identifying with others who are getting into trouble, creating a negative identity, and taking some fateful steps toward juvenile delinquency. Some kids take a measure of self-esteem from being able to successfully act in opposition to school rules and authority figures.

Too many young people do not hit it off with their peers. They have trouble exchanging information, managing conflict, and establishing a common ground of activities that they like to do with others. They do not connect on more intimate levels with others. They are more likely to tell secrets and not keep the trust of peers who could have been their good friends.

Talk to parents of hyperactive children. The behavioral excesses of these children set them on a collision course with both peers and teachers. Being fidgety, inattentive, and unable to focus on the perspectives, interests, or needs of another lead these children to be isolated on the playground, in the evenings, and on the weekends. The smooth fabric of social skills that their siblings so naturally acquire never really takes hold for them. They do not know how to competently start a conversation of mutual interest with a peer, change the topic, effectively disagree, or end the conversation in a mutually satisfying way. The neurology that drives the hyperactivity mirrors the luxury liner captain's decision to move "all ahead full," straight into the iceberg's path.

Social disaster is a daily occurrence for far too many children. We have a country full of special needs children who take problems like these with them into the workplace. The consequences of this can be seen in the widespread underemployment and unemployment of these capable and potentially productive young people. A lack of social skills competence shackles their career aspirations and achievement.

Prosocial Behavior. Helping, sharing, and caring for others headline a range of human actions in which an individual acts voluntarily to help another out. Many religious leaders, behavioral genetic researchers, and philosophers agree that humans possess an innate biological predisposition to be prosocial. Our unique prefrontal neocortex has developed in such a way that it allows us to have a conscience, act with concern for others, and be aware of our social responsibilities.

However, diverse cultural and community child-raising practices uniquely shape the expression of our ability to act prosocially. For example, Mexican American children (with a stronger ethnic identity) have shown a greater tendency to give more to peers even if that means that they will incur greater costs for themselves (Knight, Cota, & Bernal, 1993). Adults living in a kibbutz tend to be more helpful to others than adults who live in cities or even in other agricultural communities that do not have a communal philosophy (Yinon, Sharon, Azgad, & Barshir, 1981). Japanese and Chinese communities that reward group rather than individual accomplishment raise children who more often act in ways to soothe, help, and share with other children (Stevenson, 1991). Children raised in rural communities act more cooperatively with others than children reared in urban settings.

Don't get me wrong; this is both an idealistic hope and a pragmatic goal. Given the conflicts that face our world today, it is hard to argue with the idea that more prosocial actions between people couldn't hurt. However, acting prosocially on the job will also help your teenagers to achieve more pragmatic gains. For example, a study in England found that employees who held the most prestige, value, and influence in their companies were the ones whom others could come to for advice and consultation. They were the ones who could be accurately empathic and help others to express their thoughts and feelings. Acting prosocially substantially enhanced the value of these employees to their employers.

Teenagers who are appropriately assertive (able to reach that balance point between compliance and aggressiveness where they can state their opinion and be directive when necessary) are more likely to act more prosocially when confronted by difficult situations. They share, are helpful, and express sympathy with others. They are the ones who initiate and provide assistance when someone is in need. Children with a positive sense of self-esteem also are more likely to act to help others.

Prosocial children are not shy or socially anxious. While they are assertive, they are not overly competitive or aggressive with others. They are good social problem solvers and like to approach novel situations and people. They are more likely to have close friends and be esteemed in their peer group. These are qualities that will help your teenagers successfully attain valued career futures that provide meaning and purpose to their adult work life.

Diversity Skills

I hope that I have done a good job of weaving the theme of diversity throughout this book. It is an important part of each chapter. The world that your children will inherit will require them to use a range of multicultural and diversity skills if they are to be successful. Changes in the workplace mirror the dramatic demographic changes in the United States. We are now a culturally pluralistic society that is moving toward implementing the highest ideals of a truly democratic society. This means that different groups (like women and minorities) are earning their way into jobs of power and influence that have historically been closed off to them. As well, gay, lesbian, and bisexual individuals are now more visible in the workplace and are assertively demanding equal protection under the law. Your son will not only have to negotiate a satisfying relationship with a partner in his private life, but he will also likely have a woman for a boss at work (and definitely as colleagues and coworkers).

Your children will be disabled if they are unprepared, uncomfortable, or unwilling to work with others who are very different from themselves. The global marketplace knows no geographic or racial borders. Companies need individuals who can work effectively with others from different regions of the world, cultures, religions, ethnicities, and races. Businesses realize that they will be more profitable if they can liberate the full potential of each employee. One way to do this is to create a workplace that is responsive to the cultural and lifestyle differences between employees.

This extends to job sharing possibilities for both women and men who want to be home with their children for longer periods of time than a full-time job permits.

In this new era, socially competent individuals need to possess an interrelated hierarchy of diversity skills. First, they should be knowledgeable about and familiar with the differences that characterize the people they are working with and their customers. Second, they need to be comfortable working with diverse individuals. Comfort and ease allow the creation of positive working relationships between people who are markedly different from each other. Third, acceptance and respect for differences will lead to an understanding of our common humanity (paradoxically, you begin to realize that we are not all that different from each other). And finally, your children's lives will be much less if they do not experience the immense enrichment that is made possible by the differences between individuals from different racial, ethnic, cultural, and religious backgrounds. In my own experience, it seems clear to me that when we begin to appreciate and truly respect differences between individuals we catch a glimpse of the deeper connections that bind us all together into one human family.

Responsible Work Habits

"Thank you for always being on time for work" is what my oldest daughter's boss told her last week. As a special needs young adult, she has been working part time now for several months bagging groceries at a local supermarket. At times, her poor motor coordination and difficulty organizing tasks have led to a few customer complaints and some unwanted extra attention from her supervisor. However, she is rigidly dogmatic about being at work on time and never leaving her post to wander around the store (or hide out in the parking lot when she is supposed to be rounding up shopping carts, like I see some of her coworkers doing as they chat with their friends on their cell phones). This is the same child who missed only about 5 days of school throughout her 4 years in high school. And 2 of those days happened because we made her not go to school as we were leaving to visit her grandparents.

This responsible set of work behaviors has encouraged her boss to work with her to overcome the rough spots. So far the result is that not only has she been able to keep her job, but she is now getting nearly double the hours. She has a savings account with more than $3,000 in it. She doesn't like to spend her money and searches for bargains rather than part with her hard-earned dollars. These buying habits are very different from when she was tapping into Mom and Dad's cash.

How many times have you heard people say that their success was due mostly to perspiration rather than inspiration? The book I published in 2004 was the result of about 30 minutes of inspiration and then about 3 years of hard work. Completing tasks in a high-quality manner requires a sound work ethic. Do your teenagers take advantage of opportunities for extra help at school? Do they go in early or stay for extra review and practice sessions after school with their teachers? Are they concerned about doing their best on their assignments? How would you describe their work ethic?

Are your teenagers dependable? Are they on time for school and other responsibilities? Do their teachers see them as the kind of students who return promptly from breaks and get right back to work? Do they take responsibility for their actions and make good judgments? From their actions, you can begin to see how their work ethic is becoming ingrained into how they approach, manage, and engage in achievement-oriented situations at school, in your home, and when they are out in the community.

Developing an internalized orientation to be industrious is one of the greatest gifts that you can help your children acquire. As your children move through their elementary, middle school, and junior high years, their development will be incomplete and flawed if they do not experience that they can be useful and competent. These are the years in which they must learn the tasks and roles (student, worker, good citizen) that are necessary for success as an adult member of our society. Children who do not learn this will develop in brittle ways that crack under adversity or the stress of important life transitions.

Teenagers who can initiate and take risks to embrace new opportunities will be much less likely to feel inferior to others (regardless of their level of talent and ability). A very well respected 35-year longitudinal study of adults in their 20s, 30s, and 40s found that people who had incorporated a sense of personal industry into their lives during their junior high school years were much more likely as adults to have better relations with others, earn more and not be unemployed, and not exhibit emotional or antisocial problems (Vondracek, 1993). Developing a set of responsible work habits and an orientation to be industrious serves as a necessary foundation for success in whatever career field your teenagers choose to enter.

Positive Personal Qualities

How able are your teenagers to be leaders? How would you describe their work style? Are they more likely to be managers or inspirational leaders? Or are they idea generators? Perhaps they are noted for finishing projects by paying attention to details. Every successful organization has people who perform each of these vital tasks. Many people who are drawn into leadership roles are outgoing, are not afraid of competition, and value achievement. How would you describe yourself? How would you describe your teenager?

Do you like the person you have become? Do your teenagers like who they are? Having a sound overall feeling of self-esteem is a very good thing. It is easier for people who feel good about themselves to be enthusiastic about their work, to be open to learning, and to try new things. I am not suggesting that you go overboard on the self-esteem craze (as this can really be overdone), but many subtle advantages come to people who have a more positive attitude about themselves and the world around them.

Do you dress for success? How about your teenagers? Personal hygiene and appearance need to be attended to. Good grooming and cleanliness are habits best learned at home. This is a tough issue for parents, especially as children go through the adolescent years and experiment with alternative looks, dress, and styles of defining themselves. For most children, the basics of good personal hygiene can be put in place during the prekindergarten and early elementary school years. The dividends of effective early training pay off big time.

How do your teenagers present themselves when in public? Do they make eye contact with adults as they talk? Do they have the social graces to smile at the right time and make good social conversation? A more positive self-presentational style will help your teenagers connect to influential social networks that can be instrumental to their success.

Positive Personality and Emotional State

You must be ready, willing, and able to respond if your teenagers need the kind of help that can best be provided by mental health professionals. Adolescents can be overwhelmed with feelings of sadness, anxiety, and sudden changes in their moods. Sometimes this is the normal, to be expected, "storm and stress" of adolescence; at other times it is really something else. Many of the more serious mental health disorders begin to surface during the adolescent years. If left untreated, the progression of these problems in adulthood can be most destructive to your children's well-being. Early intervention is by far the best strategy. These kinds of problems have a very nasty effect on the happiness and satisfaction that your children will find in adulthood. If you have concerns about your teenagers, I encourage you to contact someone who can assist you to find the help that your family may need. Your children's school counselor or pediatrician can refer you to effective, licensed mental health care professionals in your community. Sometimes a combination of counseling and medication is the best strategy to follow. Now let me give you one example.

Social fears and social phobias will, if left untreated, hound your children's lives. Fear of public speaking is the number one phobia in the United States. Being able to make a sales pitch to a new business customer is an incredibly valuable vocational skill. Unfortunately, social phobias such as this rob adults of the ability to do such things. Social phobias can drown your teenagers in a tidal wave of fear about situations in which they excessively worry that they might be embarrassed in front of others or caught in situations from which escape is not possible. Between 3% and 13% of all adults experience some type of social fear that greatly diminishes their occupational and personal lives (American Psychiatric Association, 2000). These problems often start during the teenage years and can be related to shyness and other social difficulties in childhood.

The negative influence of shyness on career success has been well documented. Shy people tend to be overly preoccupied with themselves while interacting with others. They often fear that others will judge them to be inept, incompetent, stupid, lazy, or any number of other negative descriptors. Shy people tend to be more isolated, lonely, and lacking in a social support network of caring relationships. Others frequently describe shy people as not being as likable or as affectionate.

Shy adults avoid career paths that require frequent interpersonal exchanges, such as sales jobs. They are less likely to engage in career exploratory behaviors and critical information-seeking actions. They may be more undecided about their career direction. Their difficulties may prevent them from acting in ways that have a better chance of paying off (e.g., shy people may not agree that acting assertively in a job interview is a good thing). Shy adults have a harder time establishing and maintaining effective relationships with coworkers and supervisors.

Assertiveness training, social skills training, and working with a licensed mental health professional can help your teenagers learn more effective ways to deal with the everyday social situations they find overwhelming. A career counselor can provide a safe place for your teenagers to develop their vocational identity and engage in age-appropriate career exploratory behaviors. If you are worried about possible mental health issues that may be hurting your children, please don't wait—act now. Problems such as depression, moods cycling from lows to highs, eating disorders, and social phobias do not have to be the defining characteristic of your children's journey through adolescence and young adulthood.

Entrepreneurship

Today, to be socially competent your teenagers need to know how to think and act as entrepreneurs. Although they may never start or own their own business, these skills will benefit your teenagers in whatever career path they choose to follow. There are more than 25 million small businesses in the United States, employing about one half of our nation's private workforce. Most analysts would argue that our economic well-being is fundamentally tied to the initiative and creativity of growth-oriented small business ventures. Developing a "make your own job" attitude in your children will prepare them to enjoy some of these incredible opportunities.

Women and minorities are starting their own businesses like never before. A recent study found a huge increase in the number of businesses being started by women (Kourilsky & Walstad, 2000). Many women see the opportunity to make their own job and start their own small business as a way to more satisfactorily balance the stresses and strains of multiple role demands (parent, spouse, and worker). Since the early 1990s, African American-owned businesses have nearly doubled, and between 70% and 80% of African American and Hispanic American young people indicate an interest in one day owning and operating their own business.

Adolescents express strong interests in becoming entrepreneurs. Your teenagers will want to become entrepreneurs if they know how and have the right support to realize their dreams. Adolescents like the idea of being their own boss. They anticipate that if they work for themselves they can have more control over their lives and earn a higher income. Your teenagers probably like the idea of testing themselves and overcoming obstacles to their entrepreneurial success. Young people feel that their entrepreneurial success will build something of value for their family. Furthermore, their success will put them in a position to one day be able to help others and be of useful service to their community.

Unfortunately, several obstacles get in your teenagers' way of realizing their entrepreneurial interests. Current educational practices do not fully build on and strengthen these ambitions. Many young people do not know entrepreneurs who can serve as role models, teaching them the ins and outs and how to do its that you learn best from people who have firsthand experience. Also, teachers and school counselors do not encourage development of these interests and skills. They may not know how to do it themselves and therefore find it nearly impossible to lead young people down this career path. In my experience, when schools have a "job shadowing" day for the students, they miss a real opportunity to expose young people to the possibilities of entrepreneurship. For example, far too many students will see themselves as "sandwich makers" not "franchise owners." Helping your teenagers learn how to become small business owners is a very valuable skill for them to possess.

In Chapter 7 you and your teenagers will do an exercise in which you will visit the Ewing Marion Kauffman Foundation. You will learn more about how to become an entrepreneur, including the financial and legal issues related to owning your own business. You will begin the brainstorming process to identify entrepreneurial ideas that your teenagers could try out right now. Why wait, maybe they could create their own summer jobs! Many teenagers are already doing this.

• Conclusion •

Chapter 4 has presented you with seven targets that are crucial skills for your teenagers to master. Success in locating, entering, and progressing in a career that has meaning and purpose for your teenagers will become more likely if your adolescents engage in the present and move toward the future with proactive, resilient, and adaptive strengths (Target 1). To develop these strengths, your children need to believe in themselves (Target 2), develop effective educational and career goals (Target 3), understand themselves and the world of work (Target 4), develop and pursue their interests (Target 5), become self-regulated and successful lifelong learners (Target 6), and get along well with others, especially those who are markedly different from themselves (Target 7). Chapter 5 provides examples of high school seniors who are attempting to integrate these strengths as they engage in the present and move toward desired post–high school futures.

• Chapter 5 •
Examples

• Gina •
The Opposite of Indecisive, Pessimistic, and Immature

Student Voices

Gina is a Caucasian American woman. At the time of this interview with a school counselor, she was a senior attending a suburban high school. She is a very strong student (ranking in the top 5% of her class). A brief portion of the transcript from her Structured Career Development Interview is reported here. Gina is very committed and enthusiastic about becoming a school counselor. This valued, possible self helps to provide her with a sense of direction, purpose, and hope in her life.

Counselor: So, right now what do you think you want to do after leaving high school?

Gina: I want to go to college for 4 years to start out. I want to get some background information on schools, especially counseling, 'cause that's what I want to be when I get older is a counselor. I know counseling doesn't make a lot of money, but I just want to help people when I get older. I want a job where it's rewarding to me, not only, you know, if it's good money. I want to do something that involves helping people, you know, such as I could be doing stuff for the community or anything as long as it's benefiting someone's life or something.

Counselor: What are some of the things you are doing right now to prepare yourself to reach your career goals?

Gina: Kind of like leadership things, I'm in a group where we do stuff for the community. There are only seven or eight of us in our school who do this. I'm in Key Club, that's associated with Kiwanis, so I do all kinds of community service work. Last year I was vice president of that, and this year I'm going to be president. I can't, you know, be a real counselor right now. So the things I'm doing are the best I can do right now.

Interpretation

Gina's story offers us a glimpse of how a proactive, resilient, and adaptive approach to the present and possible career futures operates in late adolescence (Target 1). She is facing a dilemma common to most young people. High school is all but over. She is now forced to make a decision. In the timeline of her life, the choices that she makes now will greatly affect both her short- and long-term future in expected and unexpected ways. Living in our time, living in our culture, Gina is exploring possibilities that have the potential for creating an adult life that is personally meaningful and rewarding. In beginning to define what this particular something would be, she goes directly to her values.

Parents take heart; family values survive adolescence! From the developmental literature, we know that the kinds of values Gina is expressing (helping and being of service to others) are learned to a great extent at home (over the previous 18 years of her life). Even though adolescents may fight with their parents in what has been called the "storm and stress" of adolescence, your children are not likely to give up the deeper values you have taught them. In their struggle for autonomy and identity formation, adolescents may on the surface seem to reject certain family beliefs. But as you ride out these waves of conflict, the underlying values learned at home will reassert themselves.

Observational learning is one of the most effective ways in which we learn how to successfully operate in our social world. Gina attends a school that is noted for having very dynamic and caring school counselors. These counselors reach out to students and provide a service much valued by students, parents, and the school district. Studies have found that the occupational images young people embrace are (not surprisingly) those that they see around them and have some contact with (Gottfredson, 1981). This is true across different ethnic/racial groups and diverse geographic settings, from affluent suburban communities to Native American reservations (Turner & Lapan, 2003a, 2003b).

In short, Gina wants to help others and her community. She then locates an occupational form into which she can safely pour these dreams. This tentative commitment to an initial career choice (becoming a counselor) creates a goal to enter a personally valued career. This desired career identity links her actions and behavior in the present to a specific kind of future. Now, decisions that Gina has to make must be evaluated in light of their ability to bring her closer to the realization of this ideal career future. If she were not willing to put forth the effort and commitment necessary to successfully pass 4 years of college and 2 years of graduate school training, the natural consequences of these decisions would put her career dreams in jeopardy. Forging a connection between what they do in the present and a personally valued career future will help your teenagers enthusiastically and positively engage in their world.

If you talked with Gina, you would hear a tone of voice and body language that suggest hopefulness, enthusiasm, and the self-confidence to pursue a direction of her own choosing. This direction has slowly evolved due to her own explorations. When she speaks, she makes eye contact with an interviewer whom she had not met before. She leans forward to clearly express her opinions, making sure that the counselor understands her point of view. She smiles easily and makes a friendly, personal connection. If you listened to her talk about her volunteer work and newly assumed community service leadership roles, there would be absolutely no doubt in your mind that right now she is fully committed to a future direction and that she is assertively doing what she can right now to make such a future happen. How do your own teenagers talk about their future?

What you *do not* hear from Gina is a style of engaging in the present and moving toward the future that could be described as indecisive, uncertain, pessimistic, avoidant, lacking in focus, or immature. Instead, she proactively initiates and asserts control over the direction she would like her life to take. She is not a passive reactor, waiting for events to dictate a direction to her or constrain her options.

Gina is resilient. She is preparing herself for the inevitable ups and downs that entry into any career will bring. She is already identifying salary as a drawback to her career choice. She knows that there are obstacles, and if she is serious about pursuing such a direction, these problems will have to be approached with perseverance.

Gina is adapting her future plans to imbue her life with purpose and meaning. She actively explores her world and creates goals that enhance the match between the kind of person she wants to be and the different careers that would allow her to become this more ideal self.

How Would You React if Your Teenager Wanted to Be a School Counselor?

I don't know how you feel about Gina's intention to become a school counselor. Ranking in the top 5% of her class, many options will be available to her. If she were your daughter, upon hearing her decision, how would you react? How would your values and beliefs seep quickly into your facial expression and tone of voice? Would you be for it, try to talk her out of it, or remain neutral?

From my perspective, given the person that she is, the specific choice for Gina isn't what is most important right now. Without straining, I can think of many careers in which Gina could someday be highly qualified to help others and her community; for example, how about elected public official, superintendent of schools, or surgeon? There is a warehouse full of careers that will allow her to express her personal values in an occupation. She is heading off next year to a 4-year college where she will have many opportunities for new experiences and learning. Her choices will evolve and mature as she does. But whatever career decision she ultimately arrives at will be supported by this underlying behavioral approach to the world that enables her to effectively engage in the present and direct herself to valued futures.

Right now, what is crucial is that Gina has integrated a *proactive* (she has a well developed plan), *resilient* (she is ready to deal with the drawbacks and challenges that her choices lead her to), and *adaptive* (she successfully problem solves and copes with the demands and realities of formative life situations) style of engaging in everyday situations and committing herself to approach the future in a very mature way. This way of managing the present and moving toward the future will greatly increase her chances for success and satisfaction in any career that she chooses to pursue.

A big part of our job as parents is to focus on the process, while your son or daughter focuses on the goal. The particular choice isn't as important right now as establishing active and open lines of communication between you and your child. By complimenting Gina on how she is trying to find a way to enter a career that will let her express values that are important to her, we are encouraging Gina to keep exploring her options. The best way to support Gina is to talk with her in ways that let her know we are 100% behind her. Our style of communicating (rolling the eyes, taking deep breaths, being judgmental) will quickly tell her either that we trust and support her to think things through and make good decisions or that we think that she is not really able to do this critical task. We must be careful not to let our own fears and biases derail Gina's efforts to find her own way into a career that can add purpose, meaning, and a great deal of happiness to her life.

Gina believes in herself, in her ability to successfully perform specific tasks, and that she will be rewarded for her accomplishments in the future. She is rapidly resolving the identity crisis of adolescence by actively exploring her world, setting goals, and committing herself to a direction related to these goals and explorations. Gina is searching for a match between what is important in herself (such as her values) that she would need to have expressed in a career and the realities of different occupations that would allow her to utilize these essential parts of herself. Gina is eager to gather more information about colleges and related career options. How could we help her to do this? Gina is adamant that her eventual career choice will involve something about which she is deeply interested and passionate. Gina is among the top group of students in a very academically oriented high school. She has become an effective self-regulated learner. Gina automatically uses the kinds of social skills that serve as a foundation for the range of work-readiness behaviors that are integral to success in the world of work.

Conclusion

Soon you will be assessing the extent to which your own teenagers have developed this proactive, resilient, and adaptive style of engaging in the present and moving toward the future. How would you assess their growth? Could you talk to them about these issues? If so, how would you go about talking to them about this critical way of interacting in the world? Notice the kinds of statements the counselor uses when talking to Gina. You will carry on a similar conversation with your teenager using the Structured Career Development Interview in Chapter 6. In short, Gina is demonstrating competency across all seven targets.

• Shanae •
Believing in Yourself Is So Much Easier When Your Family Believes in You

Student Voices

Shanae is an African-American 12th grader attending an inner-city high school. She has a 3.5 cumulative grade point average and plans next year to attend a 4-year college to study writing. A brief portion of her Structured Career Development Interview is presented here. It highlights the very strong sense of personal self-efficacy that she possesses and the performance-enhancing adaptive attributions that she routinely makes (Target 2). Her positive efficacy beliefs and attributions are clearly linked to the support and encouragement that her parents consistently provide.

Counselor: Do the things that will help you to be successful in the future mostly come from within yourself or do they come from outside of yourself?

Shanae: I feel that it's inside and out because without my mother and father, family and stuff, I don't think I'd be in or doing anything right now. I probably wouldn't even know what I want to do with my life, so. I mean, with them I feel as long as I believe in myself, I think, I know I can do it.

Counselor: You mentioned that not getting financial aid could get in the way of reaching your goals. How are you handling this?

Shanae: I plan on, like, I'm aiming for a 4.0 all the way. I am trying to do my very best. I'll probably get a job, you know, try to help myself out, put the money in the bank and save it.

Counselor: Are you confident that you can master the educational requirements and job duties for the career you are interested in?

Shanae: Yes, because it's like it's all about time and patience, and, you know, believing that you can do it and hard work, so. Yeah, I can do it.

Counselor: After you get your education, is there anything that might get in your way from getting a satisfying job in the career you are interested in?

Shanae: No. You know, it's like, me stop believing in God. That's about it. Or me stop believing in myself.

Interpretation

Shanae believes in a golden if–then rule. If I believe in myself, then I know for certain that I can do what I need to do to be successful. As long as she feels the stability of her parents supporting her, Shanae will not doubt herself. She feels her focus, direction in life, and belief in herself to be woven into a sturdy fabric that binds her to her family. It is a shield that she places in front of her as she takes on the future. It is a resilience factor, an inoculation that she will use against the ambiguities, challenges, and unexpected twists and turns of the journey she is just beginning.

With her parents firmly behind her, Shanae will not doubt herself; they are her anchor. In the face of adversity, she knows she can count on them to bolster her belief in herself. This is the merger of "inside" and "outside" of which she speaks. It is easier to believe in yourself when you can absolutely count on the people you love to never stop believing in you.

Shanae is a very strong student, with high aspirations. She wants to go to a 4-year college and become a writer. It can be very difficult to make a living as a writer. However, the way she anticipates certain barriers to her ability to pursue her dreams tells you a lot about her chances of success. For example, she is very concerned about how she will pay for college. If you had heard her tone of voice, you would have heard a young woman speaking with the strength of personal conviction and a solid "I can do it" attitude. When she says that she is aiming to get a 4.0, as well as a job to save money, you would agree that this is a very self-determined young person who will make the future she wants happen.

Shanae uses an optimistic attribution style to understand the world she lives in. In her mind's eye, events are caused by factors that are internal, controllable, and unstable. As she says, it's about time, patience, believing you can do something, and hard work. These are factors that she can do something about. It is up to her to be patient, wait, and work hard. Whatever problems she faces, she believes she has some influence and control over them. A more pessimistic person would interpret Shanae's financial aid problems as being out of her control and impossible to change.

Shanae's self-assessment of her competence is rock solid (as long as her parents are behind her). It is a completely alien thought for her to imagine that she is not competent enough to pursue her dreams. Motivational experts have long documented how performance is enhanced from such a center of self-confidence (Target 2). She firmly believes that if she does her plan (goes to a 4-year college) then good things will inevitably happen for her. She is fortified with the confidence to assertively go after valued short- and long-range goals.

Conclusion

So now let's think about Target 2: What expectations and attributions do your teenagers use to engage in the present and move toward desired futures? Get ready, you will be talking to them very soon about this.

• Anthony •
You Need Career Goals That Work

Student Voices

Anthony is a Latino American male attending an urban high school. He is getting mostly *C*s in school. Although he says he is not at all interested in what he is currently studying in school, Anthony is very committed to someday owning his own business. The brief piece of the Structured Career Development Interview here captures these newly emerging goals, as well as a developing awareness of the kinds of people he should listen to and what he needs from others to successfully reach his goals (Target 3).

Counselor: What do you hope your future will be like?

Anthony: Plush, be comfortable, hopefully I can be set so I don't have to think about where my next piece of income is going to come from. I know people who live from check to check. They don't have a financial plan for themselves.

Counselor: What educational and career goals do you want to pursue?

Anthony: Hopefully, I can get a job this summer and then go to business school in a couple of years. I would like to get a business degree. That will help me when I open up my own business. I am starting to save some money. I'd like to own one of the small clothes stores near where I live.

Counselor: How are you preparing yourself to reach these goals?

Anthony: Well, I talked to a couple of people about some job opportunities with a bank. I know this guy who said he would help me out. I have an interview today with him.

Counselor: What challenges do you see that could get in the way of you reaching your goals?

Anthony: I am very committed to someday owning my own business. The biggest problem I see is the prejudices from everybody. 'Cause really, everyone is not out for your best interests, even your friends. So it's like, you have to listen closely to what people are telling you and decide for yourself if it's in your best interest to follow or to go your own separate way. People who give up on you, saying, I've never seen anyone do this so you're not going to be able to do this. People who don't believe in you.

Interpretation

Unfortunately, Anthony's story is an all too familiar one. He does not see the relevance of what he is studying in school to the realization of his career dreams. If you were to talk to him, you would quickly realize that this is a young man with much talent and promise. It would be a mystery for you to explain his underachievement in high school. Anthony can see a realistic future for himself in which he is both satisfied and happy. Most important, his primary goal is to achieve economic security. Unlike some of the people he knows, he does not want to live "check to check." His strategy for reaching this desired life is to become an entrepreneur. However, he anticipates that this is a career path that he will have to walk by himself.

Anthony talks freely and easily about short- and long-range goals. He had a job interview the day of this interview. He hopes to be able to save some money and then in a few years go to a business school. He believes that a business degree will help him to run the kind of small clothing store that he sees in his neighborhood and wants for himself. But there are some pieces missing. His career plans lack a certain amount of specificity and coherence.

Although he wants to someday own his own clothing store, Anthony is seeking entry-level employment in a bank. A good business to be sure, but how does he learn about owning and running his own clothing store? At some point in the distant future, he wants to go to school and get a degree in business. Anthony is a senior and will leave high school in 1 month's time, but he cannot tell you what business school he would be interested in attending (even though there are multiple options not too far from where he lives). Likewise, he cannot explain how he will pay for it. He is unaware that if he does work for a bank they probably have an employee benefits plan that could pay for at least some of his job-related education and tuition. We realize quickly that Anthony is really on his own in trying to make this happen. He has not received any substantive career counseling support from his school counselor. He is now grasping at straws to make a job happen. He is thrown back on someone he knows who said he might be able to help him out and get him a job. Listening to Anthony, we have the feeling that this is a young man walking a career tightrope without a support network.

Conclusion

The bottom line for Anthony is that he has to rely on himself if his dream is to happen. The awareness of this reality intrudes now into his thoughts and strategic planning. At the end of the day, Anthony knows that he only has his own inner strength and inner guidance to steer a course to take him where he wants to go. Even the advice of friends can't be completely trusted. They speak the language of impossibility and lack of hopefulness. To follow his divergent path, Anthony will have to be proactive, resilient, and highly adaptive (Target 1). He will have to decide not to follow the steps taken by those around him. He will have to fight off the motivation sapping belief systems that shackle initiative and change. When others think that he will amount to nothing and show him this by giving up on him, Anthony will have to believe in himself and walk his own path (Target 2). A better developed set of goals would help Anthony to sustain himself and keep on track as he makes his economic and career dreams happen (Target 3). In Chapter 7 you will have an opportunity to assess the strengths and weaknesses of both Anthony's and your teen's career goals.

• Steve •
When I Understand Myself, I Start to See My Opportunities

Student Voices

Steve is a Caucasian American high school senior living in a rural part of the United States. He has a full scholarship to attend a regional university next year. Steve plans to study chemistry and engineering, and someday work in the field of biotechnology. He hopes to be able to pursue the study of biotechnology in graduate school. He expressed very strong interests in working with ideas, things, and data. In Holland's theory that would be Investigative, Realistic, and Conventional. Steve has a very good understanding of the kinds of work tasks and work environments that would best match his talents and work values. Data from the career interview illustrate his commitment to locate and then enter a work environment that will allow him to express what is most important and valued to his sense of self (Target 4). Behind this clear sense of focus and self-confidence are parents and teachers who have consistently supported him.

Counselor: What abilities, talents, and skills do you want to use in a career?

Steve: I like problem solving. I like to hypothesize about a problem I see and then try to solve it. Kind'a like a scientific, logical approach. I have an ability to work with other people and to stay on a task, no matter how difficult it is or how long it takes me to solve it. I try to stay determined and make the best of my abilities at all times.

Counselor: What kind of working conditions would you like; for example, would you like to work indoors or outdoors?

Steve: As long as it's doing what I like and pays decent, I wouldn't really mind the environment. But my ideal place where I'd really like to work, I always wanted to work independently. You know, like those scientists who do research outdoors, out in the fields, maybe with a partner or two. They work on a problem, collect their data, and send in a report. I always wanted to do something like that.

Counselor: Have others provided you with the support you have needed to pursue these goals?

Steve: Yes, one teacher helped me to decide what to major in, what actually interested me, and what I was good at. But my parents, they are the top ones. They always have been right behind me, if I needed someone to talk to or get help from. They were always there. I'm the first generation in my family to go to college.

Interpretation

Steve lives in a midwestern state with a very large commitment to agriculture. Over the past several years, the senior U.S. Senator has championed the cause of creating a biotechnology corridor across the state. The hope is that economic development will be dramatically accelerated by the emergence of new private ventures that capitalize on this new high-tech industry. The part of the state where Steve lives has already experienced the initial wave of this business activity. He lives nearby and regularly drives past fields dedicated to a whole new agricultural enterprise that his grandparents (or parents for that matter) would never have dreamed possible. Within this political, geographic, and economic context, a specific picture of a personally valued career future is emerging for Steve. He has plenty of self-confidence, but that is not enough. Steve needs a direction to follow. This is taking shape as his perceptions of his work values, personality, abilities, and understanding of the world of work interact with the reality of the time and place in which he lives.

Look back at the work values listed in Target 4. Steve wants a career in which he can be curious and single-mindedly solve difficult problems (no matter how long he has to stay at it). He knows that he will be more satisfied if he can work to a great extent independently and outdoors. Steve wants to be economically secure and earn a "decent" living that he will define for himself (but he is not driven to find a career in which he will earn the most money possible). He wants to use his hands in his work and take advantage of the latest tools and technologies to work with plants. He is committed to pursuing a course of training that will take at least 4 years of college to complete and could lead him to one day earn a PhD. Steve is not afraid of taking intellectual risks in his work. In his geographical region, the use of biotechnology in manipulating crops is quite controversial and heatedly debated. Finally, Steve values having some autonomy and control over the work tasks and problems that he will attempt to solve.

Look back at Holland's six personality types (see Box 4.4). Three types draw a picture of a personality orientation that is critically important to Steve (Investigative, Realistic, and Conventional). Steve is a strong Investigative type. He is very curious about how and why things work. He prefers to approach the world in an analytical, scientific manner. He also has a pronounced Realistic side. He is drawn to mechanical, well-ordered tasks that need to be accomplished outdoors. Steve is also more Conventional than the average person. That is, he likes to manipulate data and keep records related to the facts that he finds. He feels more comfortable performing well-ordered tasks that take place in a clearly defined organizational hierarchy. A position as a research professor at a university would provide Steve with the autonomy he values to focus on different work problems while at the same time house him in a stable, secure, and predictable organization.

Steve has already demonstrated a wide range of abilities that could take him successfully into many different occupations. He has shown a solid general learning ability to take difficult classes in high school and get very good grades. In doing this, he has exhibited well-developed verbal and numerical skills. It would not be surprising to learn that he is proficient at spatial reasoning and data recording clerical tasks.

How satisfied would Steve be in a sales career where each day to be successful he would need to convince others to buy something? Could you imagine Steve working as an accountant in a bank? How about as a public relations spokesman for a biotechnology company? These are all careers that Steve has the ability to perform. However, they do not closely match the preferred orientations for interacting with the environment that Steve has so far developed. Maybe in time, as Steve grows and matures, he might want to become a public advocate for biotechnology. But now he is drawn to the scientific and analytical work offered by this field.

Conclusion

Do you see the important role played by significant others in the critical career decisions Steve is now making? He was extremely fortunate to have a teacher help him to recognize his talents and direct him to a possible college major that he has become most interested in pursuing. Notice the difference between the emotional and instrumental support that face some parents. Steve is the first generation in his family to go to college. Matching that to his choice of a potentially revolutionary career in biotechnology, we see that he is a real pioneer. How can his parents help him? Unlike the teacher, they may not understand the ins and outs of going to college and how their son's orientation to working outdoors and using a scientific method can lead to a college major that will connect Steve to the emerging field of biotechnology.

• Traice •
Discover Your Interests, Follow Your Passions
Student Voices

Traice describes herself as being "biracial, Black and White." She is a senior, graduating from a suburban high school. Traice is a very strong student. She has been in gifted education classes since the third grade. She has a 3.9 grade point average and earned a combined score of 1,350 on the SAT (33 on the ACT). She is planning on attending a 4-year college next year and studying English, education, and sociology. At this point in time, Traice is planning on becoming a secondary school teacher. She expresses very strong interests in working with ideas and people, and somewhat less interest in data and things (Target 5). This brief portion of her Structured Career Development Interview illustrates how Traice's career decisions are dominated by her desire to find a career that is inherently interesting and closely aligned to the kind of lifestyle she wants.

Counselor: What do you hope your future career will be like?

Traice: I'd like to have something that I really enjoy and can get wrapped up into, something that doesn't take up all of my time. I'd like to go to college for as long as I can, 'cause I like to learn, and I'm sure it will have some benefits to whatever I'll be doing. I want something that I can get up and want to go to work for. I'd want to affect people in a positive way. Right now, I think that I would like to teach in a high school.

Counselor: What kind of teacher would you like to be?

Traice: I'd like to teach writing or English or sociology. I have a lot of interests in people and why they do the things that they do, so I know in college that I will have to take a lot of child development, sociology, and psychology classes. My favorite teachers, well, they have a skill to make other people think for themselves instead of just giving them the answers.

Counselor: What careers have you already explored?

Traice: I looked into computer programming and networking, and I found out that, at least for right now, teaching will let me do more things that I really like to do.

Interpretation

There are 12 words that, when strung together and spoken matter of factly by their children, parents should come to truly fear. Each word itself is nice, friendly, and quite manageable. However, when they are spoken in a tone that tells you that your child is comfortable and not concerned about this situation, then you are in trouble! Of all the things Traice just said, what do you think I am talking about? The dreaded 12-word phrase is, "I'd like to go to college for as long as I can."

Don't get me wrong; I mostly loved the 6 years I spent doing my doctoral degree. I agree that learning is good for its own sake and doesn't necessarily need a vocational payoff. However, as a parent thinking of how to pay for three daughters to go to college, I think a little focus and direction is a good thing (a very good thing!). I don't want my kids' college experiences to look like the slow, zigzagging path of the Mississippi River as it meanders on its 2,000-mile trek to the ocean. I would like to retire someday.

Since elementary school Traice has participated in gifted education courses. Her grade point average, class rank, and SAT/ACT scores all indicate that this is a young woman with a wide range of talents. Traice's test scores qualify her for a $3,000 "bright flight" state scholarship designed to entice strong students to stay in state for college. Traice has a preference for college majors that fall into technical and artistic areas. Her interest profile most closely matches people who work in career paths related to the social sciences and computer programming/systems analysis.

How well do you think Traice's plan to teach high school matches her? Do you see any potential problems with this choice? Look again at her interests. What kind of work environment do high school teachers find themselves in? Please understand that I am not making any value judgments; if anything I wish many more young people like Traice would go into teaching. However, one concern I have for Traice is that she is more interested in thinking about people ("why they do the things they do"). Teaching certainly has some of that but is largely an environment with work tasks that will engage her in intensive and extensive interpersonal exchanges (helping, informing, and persuading). One challenge for her will be to integrate her talents and interests in social science and technical activities into her career path.

Traice's decision about what to pursue after high school is dominated by the interests that are most salient to her at this point in her life. She is sure of only one thing. She has to have a career that she "can get wrapped up into." Work that is satisfying, is meaningful, and helps to provide a sense of purpose to life flows from deep engagement in everyday tasks that are intrinsically motivating to the individual. What seems most interesting to Traice right now is a theme that is dictated by her values. Traice wants to work in a career in which she can "affect people in a positive way" and that provides her the opportunity to have some balance between work, home, and leisure activities (as she says, "something that doesn't take up all of my time").

An unspoken yet potentially huge issue for Traice is her biracial and bicultural being. She is embedded in a family that is culturally, ethnically, and racially diverse. If I were Traice's parent, I would want to talk to her about these issues and how they have helped to shape her identity. Racial identity development may be an important factor for Traice in shaping the career decisions that she makes. For example, in talking to Traice further, we might find out that when she speaks about affecting people in a positive way she really means that she wants to help people from diverse backgrounds learn how to value, embrace, benefit from each other, and learn how to live together with respect and peace. Her own biracial identity may have tuned her into the urgency of these issues. If so, her career identity has an important foundation in her identity development as both a Black and a White woman.

You shouldn't underestimate the power of these issues for your own children. For example, women readily go into the biological sciences but not into physics. Many of these women believe that by committing themselves to biology they are striving to create a better world, a healthier environment that will nurture everyone. They do not see how such a value can be realized in the pursuit of physics. Identity-shaping values can regulate how interested your child will be in a field, regardless of his or her abilities, talents, and skills.

Conclusion

To help your children with these issues, think of these three components (awareness, knowledge, and skills). These are important parts of what has come to be known as a multiculturally competent approach to counseling (Sue & Sue, 2002). First, become aware of yourself in this situation. Be open to learning about your own cultural beliefs, values, and biases. Second, try to become knowledgeable about how these issues affect your child and ultimately influence her or his career identity development. Finally, by committing yourself to communicating with your child about these issues, you are putting yourself on a path to learn the skills you will need to be helpful to your child. In discussing the family career genogram in Chapter 7, I hope you and your teen will have a wonderful opportunity to explore some of these far-reaching issues.

• Kim •

Become a More Successful Student and Lifelong Learner

Student Voices

Kim is an Asian-American senior attending a suburban high school. Through funding from the School-to-Work Opportunities Act of 1994, his school was able to implement a community career partnership. Since then, school personnel (principals, teachers, and counselors), business and community leaders, and parents have worked together to create unique learning opportunities for students (Target 6). These experiences enable juniors and seniors to connect some of their learning to possible career paths that they might want to pursue after graduating from high school. Kim's academic performance and motivation to improve himself have been substantially enhanced by participating in this academic curriculum. His high school studies are organized around a broad career path and set of goals. Kim sees the relevance to what he is studying in high school and what he will likely be doing after leaving high school. This has clearly helped him to initiate and sustain self-directed and self-regulating strategies to take control of his learning and more fully maximize the talents he possesses.

Counselor: What do you hope your future will be like?

Kim: Productive, prosperous, and fun. Fun would be nice. I will become a doctor or some other thing in the medical field.

Counselor: How are you preparing yourself to reach these goals?

Kim: I have taken HRP, which is health-related professions, and it has introduced me to the nursing career, which is what I am going to get my undergraduate degree in. I recently just got my CNA, certified nurses assistant license, and uh, hopefully this summer I will get to work in a hospital or something like that.

Counselor: What academic skills are you developing that will help you reach your career goals?

Kim: I have a 3.25 grade point average. That is a smidge low for the nursing school that I want to go to next fall. My ACT score was 24, and I think that I need to bring that up.

Counselor: Are you interested in what you are studying in school?

Kim: Yeah! I am getting A's in my science classes, and next quarter I get to take an anatomy class. At first I didn't think that I would like this stuff, but last year third quarter we went to a nursing home and, at first, it was like, no way. There is no way that I can clean up some old person's poop and stuff. But it's not as hard as I thought it was going to be, as long as you maintain a professional attitude it's great. So, I love the people up there and they love me. It's been great. I think I learned some things about myself and found out that medicine may be for me.

Interpretation

Infusing career development experiences into your teenagers' academic curriculum can enhance the process through which they will become successful and satisfied adults. The learning opportunities in the world of work provided to Kim have given him the chance to experience what it is like to have adultlike responsibility. He knows that he is doing something of importance in a context in which his behavior counts for something real; others depend on him. Caring for elderly patients challenged him to do more, to be a different kind of person. When he met this challenge, he enhanced his self-confidence. This success acted as a springboard from which he is now propelled to attack his academic learning.

Up to this point in his academic career, Kim has not been a top student. Many of you will recognize this pattern (you might see it in your own children). Kim does well in the courses that interest him and slides by in others that hold little value for him. The work world experiences that he has had have helped to make his studies relevant to him. He sees a valued future that he wants very much to pursue that is connected to what he studies and how he does in high school. He knows he has to raise his grade point average and standardized test scores if he is going to be able to do what he wants to do. The nursing school he is interested in attending is selective. He needs to improve himself if this is going to be a reality for him.

Many high schools now help students to organize their course of studies around broad career pathways. Kim is taking a sequence of courses identified in the school's curriculum as "Health-Related Professions." This is a broad area of study in which students can take courses that could lead to a wide variety of careers (medical doctor, nursing, child-care worker, or X-ray technician). The value for Kim is that this career pathway allows him to connect what he is learning to a future that he sees as meaningful and highly desirable. Are your teen's academic courses linked in any meaningful way to a personally valued career future? In the mutuality exercise in Chapter 7, you will have an opportunity to explore this topic with your teenager.

Kim is very committed to having a career in the medical field. The exploration of real-world work situations has helped him to more specifically define his career goals. Take a look back at the Top 10 characteristics of effective career goals (see Box 4.2). How would you rate Kim's career goals?

I would see it this way. Kim is firm about his interest in becoming a nurse. Although this could change, at this point in time he is very committed to this direction. It is a possible future that he is choosing on his own to pursue. The goal has become both clear and specific. While it will challenge him, it is also very attainable. This goal gives Kim assistance in orienting himself now that he is in a critical decision-making point in his life. This goal also identifies actions he can take to bring the process more under his control, such as improving his grade point average. Kim can go after this goal in his daily life. It is quite realistic for him. He also can garner the support and resources from others that he will need to reach this goal. I would give him a 10 out of 10 for his career goal. How did you rate him?

Now be honest, how do you feel about Kim becoming a nurse? How would you feel if your son wanted to become a nurse? Didn't we all laugh when Ben Stiller in *Meet the Parents* tried to explain to his future father-in-law (Robert DeNiro) why he chose nursing as a career over a career as a medical doctor? Nursing has two things going against it for Kim. One is that it is a career that we understand to be of much lower prestige than being a medical doctor (and it pays a lot less). Two, it has traditionally been a career dominated by women.

How will your own gender-role attitudes affect your reaction to your son's or daughter's career aspirations and choices? If your son said to you that he wanted to be a nurse, what would the look on your face say to him? If your daughter said to you that she wanted to be a pilot for a major airline, would the corners of your mouth go up or down?

What do you see in Kim's answers and behaviors that would lead you to think of him as a self-regulated learner? Look at how motivated and purposive he has become in his actions. Kim embodies an optimistic, forward-looking, success orientation. Do you have any doubts that he will be successful in the future, whatever he ends up choosing? He is not beset with self-doubts. Nor does he avoid challenges. He sets high standards for himself and is willing to risk engagement in a process that could lead to success or failure.

Kim is very committed to do his very best. He sees himself doing high-quality work in school. This kind of effort can make up for other shortcomings. For example, Kim may be a slower reader than the other students in his anatomy class. He may have difficulty decoding letters and words. His attitude would lead him to redouble his efforts to stick with the reading and not give up. Kim's learning is about mastery and self-improvement. He is not afraid to make a mistake in front of others, and he doesn't have to outdo everyone in his class. Kim has a goal that dictates a level of performance that he needs to reach.

If things don't go well for Kim, how would he interpret this failure? It would take a lot of adversity for Kim to really slam himself. He would be more likely to attribute difficulties to things he can control (like effort).

If Kim doesn't know something that he is reading or learning in class, what do you think he does about it? Does he keep plodding through, getting less and less from what he is learning? Or does he realize he doesn't know what is going on and try to do something about it?

If we were to show Kim a strategy for organizing a project he was working on or a mnemonic image that would help him remember a list of terms or a critical process, would he actively employ this tactic? My guess is that Kim's motivation to succeed and active engagement in his learning would lead him to embrace any strategy that he thought would improve his performance. How about your teenagers?

Conclusion

Do you see the self-fulfilling cycle that Kim is on? He is on a very positive roll. Kim sees the outcome of his efforts, a 3.25 grade point average. He takes this information and infuses it into the planning phase of his upcoming learning activities. He sets challenging goals for himself to reach a level of performance that he needs to achieve if he is going to successfully realize his valued career goals. This preparation will likely enhance his performance for the remainder of his senior year and lead to a higher grade point average. His senior year is not a time to take it easy. It is a time to improve so he can do what he really wants to do next year. What does your daughter or son need to do to become a self-regulated, successful lifelong learner?

• Tammy •
Getting Along With Others Is Money in the Bank

Student Voices

Tammy is a Caucasian American senior attending a rural high school. She gets mostly *B*s and *C*s in her classes. Tammy is planning to attend a community college next year and eventually pursue a career in law enforcement. She is well liked by both teachers and peers (Target 7). Tammy is warm, polite, and respectful of others. She makes good eye contact, answers questions in a confident and assertive manner, and is very responsible. Her social competence creates an atmosphere that encourages others to spend time with her and quickly come to trust her.

Counselor: Are you a senior?
Tammy: Yes, sir.
Counselor: What do you hope your future will be like?
Tammy: Rewardful, happy, and full of excitement.
Counselor: How do you get along with others, like teachers, peers, and parents?
Tammy: I'm a people person. I get along with my parents. I'm the baby in the family and, uh, I get along great with my parents. I tell my parents everything. I get along with my teachers

real good too. I have lots of friends. I don't look at people just because of who they are and decide if I want to talk to them. When my friends get into fights over silly stuff, I'm the moderator and I let them talk it out.

Counselor: How would you describe your work habits?

Tammy: I think that I have a good work ethic because when I turned 16 I got a job at our big super center department store. I still work there, and I can pretty much do every job at that place.

Counselor: So you are pretty resourceful?

Tammy: Yes, sir.

Counselor: How do you get along with people who have very different backgrounds from your own?

Tammy: I try not to look at people's background and just treat everyone equally.

Interpretation

I wish you could hear how Tammy handled herself in this interview and the style of engagement she uses to take charge of this interview with an adult she has not met before. Tammy is a very socially competent high school senior. She has a refined set of social skills, senses the importance of and welcomes opportunities to interact with people different from herself, uses a mature set of work habits and positive personal qualities to manage her in-school and out-of-school responsibilities, and handles herself with an assertiveness and emotional balance that entices others to want to spend more time with her.

Tammy is not a spectacular student. She is a solid student, getting mostly *B*s and *C*s in her courses. However, she possesses an exquisite ability to get along with others. Her social skills create exchanges with both peers and adults that are warm, friendly, and respectful. But she is no pushover. Tammy is the assertive leader of her friendship group. Her body language and eye contact let you know that this is a person of strength who can be counted on to make good decisions and help others out when needed. She is the mediator for conflicts in her peer group.

Tammy is very open to people who are different from her in culture, race, or religion. With additional life experiences, it is easy to imagine that when she is a working adult she will be open to learning about people with different backgrounds and act with respect, be accepting, and enjoy the enrichments to life brought about by these differences. She likes people, and people like her.

Already in her young life Tammy has demonstrated that she possesses and uses a responsible set of work habits. She has had a part-time job for the past 2 years. She can tell you about the half dozen or so different jobs that she has successfully performed at the large super center department store where she works. Tammy is the kind of employee you would love to have work for you. She is industrious and initiates actions to solve problems. She is not reactive and dependent. She does not always wait, needing constantly to be told what to do. She can be counted on to show up for work on time, and she is ready to get back to work after her breaks. Her grooming and personal hygiene practices contribute to the attractive self-presentational style that firmly cements her social connections. She is enthusiastic in her part-time job and goes after it with a positive attitude that is infectious. Whatever career she ends up going into, there is no doubt that Tammy will be a leader who will enhance the climate and quality of life in that work environment.

Tammy is blessed with a personality that radiates what has been termed "positive affectivity." She is optimistic, able to see the good in people and situations, happy with herself, and able to act assertively when the situation calls for it. She is not inundated with feelings of self-doubt, anxiety, or depression. She feels the good and bad in her life and is realistic about her situation. This balance of emotion and personality rests on a foundation of solid connections with others.

What about entrepreneurship? Do you think Tammy is able or would like to someday own her own business? She likes excitement and challenge (she is thinking now about going into law enforcement). But in an hour interview about her future aspirations, she never once mentioned that she would like to start her own business. To me, this is a big problem. It really requires a mindset change on the part of educators, counselors, and parents. Someone like Tammy has all the natural talents to be a great entrepreneur. What she lacks are learning environments that encourage and cultivate these possibilities. Young people need learning experiences to open up this vista for them. If you don't have a parent or family friend who runs his or her own business, it is very difficult to imagine yourself in such a work role. I am not suggesting that Tammy should become an entrepreneur. But I do wonder how many young people would love to challenge themselves by making their own job if they were helped to know how to do this. They need learning experiences that begin to bring this picture into focus, to see the outlines of what is both necessary and possible.

Conclusion

Tammy radiates social competence. Her communication skills are first-rate. She genuinely cares for others and is enriched by diversity. Tammy demonstrates initiative and dependability in work situations. She acts as a leader and has a foundation rooted in positive self-esteem. Tammy is not beset with problems related to anxiety, depression, or anger. The Structured Career Development Interview in Chapter 6 will help you talk to your teens about these vital work readiness behaviors.

• Conclusion •

In Chapter 6 you will learn how to use the Structured Career Development Interview with your son or daughter. It builds on the knowledge you have learned in Chapters 4 and 5. You will interview your teenager, graph the results from this interview, and then talk to your child about what this means for him or her. This will put you in a great position to actively engage your teenager in the mutual activities exercises (such as Find the Right College) presented in Chapter 7.

• Chapter 6 •
Assessments

The Structured Career Development Interview provides a strategy for you to assess how well your son or daughter is developing his or her ability to be proactive, resilient, and adaptive. It is an opportunity for you and your teenager to have a successful conversation about career issues that are important to him or her. Instructions have been provided that will take you through this process from beginning to end. Please read them carefully and closely follow them.

• Getting Ready for the Structured Career Development Interview •

To make this a true collaboration, you will first need to get buy-in from your teenager. Review material in Part One of this book about developing a working alliance with your teenager and using good listening skills. The goal is to engage your teen in a 30-minute conversation about career exploration and planning using the open-ended questions provided by the Structured Career Development Interview. Then you will score your teen's responses to these questions and complete the Career Development Profile, which graphically displays this information. Finally, I will show you how to interpret the results so you can discuss what they mean with your teenager.

Set the Stage

Okay, now let's get started. First, explain to your teenager what you are up to, stressing collaboration and the fact that these are issues your son or daughter also may be concerned about. Do not approach your teenager in an authoritarian manner (You know, the bossy I know what's best and I am here to tell you all about it attitude!). This is not about you demonstrating your power and control over how your teenager spends her or his time. This is about believing in your teen and affirming his or her inherent ability and desire to chart a personally meaningful course of action toward the future.

Calmly and kindly explain to your teenager that you would like to spend about 30 minutes talking about what he or she wants to do in the future, focusing on his or her educational goals and career dreams. Emphasize that this will enable you to start thinking about how you can help her or him and how the family is going to pull together to make these dreams become a reality. Everyone has a big stake in this.

It is fair to tell your teenagers that their chances for happiness and satisfaction will be improved if you all work together. Affirm your faith in your teenagers and their ability to make really good decisions. Be very clear that you are not going to push your views or make decisions for them. Tell your teenagers that you know they are perfectly capable of making their own decisions about their future. However, you would like to provide support as they think about issues that are very important to their future success. Let your teenagers know very clearly that, in your best judgment, not doing something like this now could really cost everyone a great deal in the future.

Use your good listening skills to really hear your teenager's reactions. This is an opportunity for you to demonstrate that you are there as a listener and supporter. You are not trying to control your teenager and will not take over the process. This is something that you both will work on together, always having a picture in mind of what the benefits to your teen will be.

Negotiate a time for your conversation. Be open to what might work. Maybe you could go out for ice cream, sit outside on a nice day, or put some background music on. Make it inviting. But don't leave any doubt in your teenager's mind that this is important business and that you want to spend some time talking seriously about these things. When you agree on a time, write it on the calendar and make sure you keep the appointment.

Some adolescents can be resistant and oppositional about anything. My experience with my own children and working with some wonderful (but, at times, highly oppositional) high school students is that they will not only agree to do this but they may even like it (although they probably won't tell you that). You have an important stake in all of this. If your motivation and resolve start to wane, talk to parents who are paying tens of thousands of dollars for college tuition bills that they know are not taking their teenager anywhere. Believe in yourself and be persistent. If you hear a little bit of a dictator creep into your voice, be careful. Your teenager will also hear it and may feel the need to fight back. This is about cooperation. Both sides, parents and teenagers, working together to benefit tomorrow's adults. Now take a few minutes to go through the dress rehearsal. It will help you to focus in on what the career interview is all about.

Dress Rehearsal

First, take a moment to relax. Slowly, take a deep breath in through your nose. Continue inhaling as you count for 5 seconds. Let the air fill up your chest and lungs. Then hold your breath for a count of 5 seconds. Now, as you count for 5 seconds, exhale through your mouth in a calm and relaxed manner. Let the air go completely out. Enjoy this feeling of deep relaxation. Repeat this process five times.

Clear your mind of whatever tasks or hassles you may need to deal with today. Focus only on your son or daughter. Think about how you see your teenager relating to others at home. What do you hear about your teenager when he or she is in school? How does your teenager behave out in the community alone, with another family, or with friends?

What does your teenager do? Does your teen have a part-time job, do community service work, play a sport, act in a theater group, or play a musical instrument? Whatever it might be, how does your teenager interact in these settings? As you let these images float to the surface, think about the following questions. Does your daughter or son

1. interact with a sense of purpose and direction, having some kind of a picture of a valued future that she or he is interested in moving toward?
2. effectively pursue valued opportunities and choices?
3. act with assertiveness and personal initiative?
4. exhibit a mature commitment to a self-defined direction?
5. act in hopeful, motivated, and optimistic ways?
6. persevere to overcome obstacles?
7. turn unexpected events into positive opportunities?
8. explore the world, demonstrating both curiosity and creativity?
9. show a tendency to be entrepreneurial (someone who might one day make her or his own job)?
10. get along with and care for others?

These are not easy questions to answer. They take some time to think about, but your teenager is worth it. Take a few minutes and write down your thoughts. If it would be helpful, find another adult you can talk to about these issues. Discuss what you are thinking and feeling about your own teenager. This should help you to gain some insight and perspective as you do the Structured Career

Development Interview with your teenager. Enjoy this, have some fun with it. This is a great opportunity to focus in on someone you love very much!

Directions for Parents

Now it is time to have a conversation with your son or daughter about his or her educational and career plans. Remember to create the right tone and feeling for this meeting. You and your teenager are collaborators. You will ask your teenager a series of open-ended questions. Each question taps into the central core of the seven targets (Chapter 4) and seven examples (Chapter 5) you have just read about. After you ask each question, try to get your teenager to explore it in some depth. You do this by using your good listening skills. Make sure you know and can effectively use the communication skills described in Part One and in the Appendix. Remember, your goal is to gather as much information as possible so that you can make a solid assessment. In the spaces provided, write down some of the important ideas that your teenager talks about. Use your good listening skills to assist your teenager to more fully explore his or her thoughts and feelings about each question.

• Structured Career Development Interview •

Start by filling out some basic information about your teenager.

Name ______________________________ Sex _____ Age _______ Date_________

Grade _____ School ____

Next, say the following to your daughter or son:

> I am going to ask you a few questions. I would like us to be able to explore together what you think about these issues. There are no "right" or "wrong" answers to these questions. The questions deal with your thoughts about your future, your plans to pursue educational opportunities and enter a satisfying and rewarding career. It is important that you give your honest opinion and that your answers reflect how you really feel and think about your future plans and choices. I am going to write down some of the important ideas that you talk about so we can discuss them later. It is really okay if you don't have an answer for some of these questions. These are things we just need to learn more about. Let's take our time and talk through these questions together.

Being Proactive and Setting Effective Goals

1. What do you hope your *future* will be like?

   ____

   ____

   ____

2. What *educational* and *career plans* would you like to pursue in the future?

   ____

   ____

   ____

3. Right now, how are you *preparing* yourself to achieve these goals?

   ____

   ____

   ____

4. How *committed* are you to these plans? Are they likely to *change*?

   ____

   ____

   ____

5. How are you being *assertive* in going after these opportunities?

6. Are you *hopeful* that you will someday work in a career where you will be *happy* and *satisfied*?

Having Positive Expectations

1. How *confident* are you in your ability to successfully deal with challenges you may face in reaching your educational and career goals? Tell me why you think you either *have* the self-confidence needed to reach these goals or *do not have* enough self-confidence.

2. What *challenges* do you see in front of you?

3. Are these challenges *easily fixed* or more *difficult* to resolve?

4. What *strategies* will you use to deal with these challenges?

5. Do you have any *concerns* about your ability to master the educational skills and job duties required by your educational and career goals?

6. After you are successful in preparing yourself to enter a career, what things might *get in your way* and prevent you from getting a satisfying job in that career (for example, you might be worried that there wouldn't be many job openings in that field)?

Knowing Yourself

1. What *abilities, talents,* and *skills* do you want to use in a future career? What kinds of careers would be more likely to let you use these abilities, talents, and skills?

2. What *work values* (such as being creative, earning a high income, being your own boss, helping others, and so forth) are important to you? What kinds of careers would be more likely to let you express these values in your work?

3. What aspects of your *personality* (such as enjoying working alone or working with others) do you want to use in a future career? What kinds of careers would be more likely to encourage you to use these parts of your personality?

4. What kinds of careers *interest* you? What is it about them that you find interesting?

5. What kinds of *work conditions* (like working indoors or outdoors) would you like to have in a career? What kinds of careers would be more likely to have these kinds of work conditions?

6. What kinds of careers would best *match* who you are and what you are looking for in a career? With all the choices that are available, where in the world of work do you think you best *fit*?

Becoming a Successful Student

1. What *academic skills* are you developing to help you reach your educational and career goals?

2. Are your *grade point average* and *test scores* where you need them to be to reach your goals? Please explain.

3. How are you doing in your *language arts* classes? What plans do you have to take *additional* and advanced coursework in this area (like honors or advanced placement courses)?

4. How are you doing in your *mathematics* classes? What plans do you have to take *additional* and advanced coursework in this area (like honors or advanced placement courses)?

5. How are you doing in your *science and technology* classes? What plans do you have to take *additional* and advanced coursework in this area (like honors or advanced placement courses)?

6. Are you *interested* in what you are studying in school? Please explain. If you are not interested in your current classes, what would you be interested in learning about?

Getting Along With Others

1. How do you *communicate* and *get along* with others (such as teachers, friends, or an employer if you have one) and build good relationships? For example, do you use good listening skills, speak up and assertively state your opinion, and do you listen to the feelings and perspectives of others?

2. How do you get along with people who have very *different backgrounds* from your own (such as people who are ethnically or racially different from you)? Could you describe some examples?

3. How would you describe your *work habits*?
   a. Do you initiate actions to solve problems?

   b. Do you have a good work ethic and complete tasks on time?

   c. Can teachers, coaches, or a boss count on you to be responsible and dependable?

   d. Can you work well with others as part of a team to complete school projects and solve difficult problems?

4. Are you or could you be a positive leader at school? If so, how are you being a leader? If not, what stops you from becoming a leader?

5. Do feelings of fear, sadness, shyness, or anger sometimes bother you and get in your way?

____
____
____

6. Would you like to someday *own your own business*? Have you ever thought about it?

____
____

   a. Do you know some of the things that are involved in owning your own business? If so, what?

   ____
   ____
   ____

   b. Would you like to learn more about how to start and run your own business?

   ____
   ____
   ____

Following Your Interests

Work tasks can be organized into four categories: working with *data,* working with *ideas,* working with *people,* and working with *things.* Read the work task descriptions that follow and then circle 0, 1, or 2 to record your teenager's ratings of his or her interest in data, ideas, people, and things work activities.

1. *Data work tasks* include working with facts, records, files, and numbers. Data activities have you record, verify, transmit, and organize facts and data to get goods and services to customers. Some data careers are purchasing agents, accountants, and air traffic controllers. How *interested* are you in doing *data* work tasks in a career?

   0 Low level of interest
   1 Medium level of interest
   2 High level of interest

   Your son's or daughter's DATA Score = ___

2. *Ideas work tasks* include abstractions, theories, knowledge, insights, and finding new ways of expressing something (for example, through the use of words, pictures, mathematics equations, or music). Ideas activities have you create, discover, interpret, synthesize, and implement these abstractions. Some ideas careers are scientists, musicians, and writers. How *interested* are you in doing *ideas* work tasks in a career?

   0 Low level of interest
   1 Medium level of interest
   2 High level of interest

   Your daughter's or son's IDEAS Score = ___

3. *People work tasks* and activities include working with others to help them, inform them, serve them, persuade them, entertain them, direct them, and motivate them. Some people careers are teachers, salespersons, and nurses. How *interested* are you in doing *people* work tasks in a career?

   0 Low level of interest
   1 Medium level of interest
   2 High level of interest

   Your son's or daughter's PEOPLE Score = ___

4. *Things work tasks* include working with machines, mechanisms, materials, tools, as well as physical and biological processes. Things activities have you produce, transport, service, and repair things. Some things careers are electricians, technicians, and engineers. How *interested* are you in doing *things* work tasks in a career?

   0 Low level of interest
   1 Medium level of interest
   2 High level of interest

   Your daughter's or son's THINGS Score = ___

5. Have you *actively explored* data, ideas, people, or things work tasks involved in a variety of careers? If yes, what have you done, and what specific careers have you learned about?

   ____

   ____

   ____

Congratulations! You have now finished the Structured Career Development Interview. Please thank your teenager for doing this interview with you. Let your teen know that you would like to talk to him or her later about the results. Take a few minutes to relax and review the information you have just gathered. When you are ready, proceed to the next section and score your teenager's interview.

• • •

• Scoring Your Teenager's Interview •

Using the information you have gathered from both your Structured Career Development Interview with your teenager and your observations of how he or she acts in important social situations (like school), answer the following questions. Circle 0, 1, or 2, depending on your best assessment of how your teenager is developing these critical life skills. Record your score for each question in the space provided after every six questions. Finally, add your ratings together to get your Total Score for each section, and put that number in the space provided.

Being Proactive, Resilient, and Adaptive

1. *Direction:* Can your son or daughter describe an educational or career direction that he or she really wants to go after?

   0 *No*
   My teen has trouble talking about any educational or career options that he or she wants to go after.
   1 *Somewhat*
   My teen can somewhat talk about an educational or career option that he or she wants to go after.
   2 *Yes*
   My teen can talk with some understanding and specific information about an educational and career option that he or she really wants to go after.

2. *Commitment:* Is your son or daughter committed to pursuing a specific educational and career path?

   0 *No*
   My teen has not made any decisions about pursuing an educational and career path.
   1 *Somewhat*
   My teen is considering some educational and career options but is not yet firmly committed to them.
   2 *Yes*
   My teen has made a decision to pursue an educational and career path and is firmly committed to it.

3. *Preparation:* Is your son or daughter actively preparing to achieve future educational and career goals?

   0 *No*
   At best, my teen is only beginning to think about doing what needs to be done to achieve future educational and career goals.
   1 *Somewhat*
   My teen is actively doing some things to achieve future educational and career goals.
   2 *Yes*
   My teen has given serious thought to and has actively done several things to achieve future educational and career goals.

4. *Initiative:* Does your son or daughter show initiative and take advantage of opportunities that will help him or her to successfully reach future educational and career goals?

   0 *No*
   My teen does not show initiative nor take advantage of opportunities.
   1 *Somewhat*
   My teen sometimes shows initiative and takes advantage of opportunities.
   2 *Yes*
   My teen frequently shows initiative and takes advantage of opportunities.

5. *Assertiveness:* Does your son or daughter assertively take charge of things and do what needs to be done to successfully reach future educational and career goals?

   0 *No*
   My teen is not assertive in pursuing future educational and career goals.
   1 *Somewhat*
   My teen demonstrates some assertiveness in pursuing future educational and career goals.
   2 *Yes*
   My teen is very assertive in pursuing future educational and career goals.

6. *Hopefulness:* Is your son or daughter hopeful that one day he or she will work in a career in which your teen will be happy and satisfied?

   0 *No*
   My teen is not very hopeful that this will happen for him or her.
   1 *Somewhat*
   My teen is somewhat hopeful that this will happen for him or her.
   2 *Yes*
   My teen is very hopeful that this will happen for him or her.

Being Proactive = ___ + ___ + ___ + ___ + ___ + ___ = _____ ***Total Score***

Question 1, 2, 3, 4, 5, 6

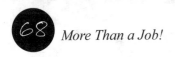

Having Positive Beliefs

1. *Self-Efficacy for Challenges and Barriers:* Is your son or daughter confident in his or her ability to successfully deal with challenges he or she may face when attempting to reach future educational and career goals?

   0 *No*
   My teen is not confident in her or his ability to successfully deal with these challenges.

   1 *Somewhat*
   My teen is somewhat confident in her or his ability to successfully deal with these challenges.

   2 *Yes*
   My teen is very confident in her or his ability to successfully deal with these challenges.

2. *Self-Efficacy for Educational Requirements and Job Duties:* Is your son or daughter confident that he or she could successfully master both the educational requirements and the job duties necessary to work in careers that really interested him or her?

   0 *No*
   My teen expresses significant self-doubt in his or her ability to successfully master educational requirements and job duties of desired careers.

   1 *Somewhat*
   My teen is somewhat confident in his or her ability to successfully master educational requirements and job duties of desired careers.

   2 *Yes*
   My teen is very confident in his or her ability to successfully master educational requirements and job duties of desired careers.

3. *Outcome Expectations:* If your son or daughter were to successfully prepare to enter a career that interested him or her, does your teen believe there are things that would get in the way of actually getting a satisfying job in that career?

   0 *Yes*
   My teen expects that her or his career plans may not really work out even if she or he successfully prepares for them.

   1 *Somewhat*
   My teen is somewhat concerned that her or his career plans may not really work out even if she or he successfully prepares for them.

   2 *No*
   My teen expects that her or his career plans will work out if she or he successfully prepares for them.

4. *Locus Attributions:* Does your son or daughter believe that the important things that will really help him or her to be successful in reaching educational and career goals come mostly from inside (such as personal talents and effort) or from outside events (such as support others may or may not provide or chance events and luck)?

   0 *Mostly external*
   The important things come from events that are outside of my teen.

   1 *Somewhat internal*
   The important things come from a source somewhat internal to my teen.

   2 *Mostly internal*
   The important things come from sources that are mostly internal to my teen.

5. *Stability Attributions:* Does your son or daughter believe that the problems that could get in the way as he or she tries to reach educational and career goals will be hard to solve or fairly easy to solve?

   0 *Problems are mostly permanent in nature*
   My teen believes that these problems can't really be resolved.
   1 *Problems can be solved but with some difficulty*
   My teen believes these problems can be fixed but that it will be difficult to do so.
   2 *Problems can be relatively easily solved*
   My teen believes that these problems are relatively easy to fix.

6. *Control Attributions:* Does your son or daughter believe that the causes of potential problems that could get in the way as he or she tries to reach educational and career goals are due to forces that your teen can or cannot control?

   0 Causes of problems are due to forces that my teen *can't control.*
   1 Causes of problems are due to forces that my teen *can somewhat control.*
   2 Causes of problems are due to forces that my teen *can to a great extent control.*

Having Positive Beliefs = ___ + ___ + ___ + ___ + ___ + ___ = _____ ***Total Score***
Question 1 2 3 4 5 6

Creating Effective Goals

1. *Specific and Clearly Defined Goals:* Are your son's or daughter's educational and career goals clear and specific?

   0 *No*
   My teen's educational and career goals are unclear and very general.
   1 *Somewhat*
   My teen's educational and career goals are somewhat defined and specific.
   2 *Yes*
   My teen's educational and career goals are clearly defined and specific.

2. *Difficult and Challenging Goals:* Are the educational and career goals your son or daughter has chosen appropriately difficult and challenging?

   0 *No*
   The goals my teen has chosen either are much too difficult or are not challenging enough.
   1 *Somewhat*
   The goals my teen has chosen will be somewhat difficult and challenging to reach. However, I am concerned that the difficulty level and challenges my teen will face in reaching these goals do not closely match my teen's abilities and talents.
   2 *Yes*
   The goals my teen has chosen will be appropriately difficult and challenging to reach. I believe the difficulty level and challenges my teen will face in reaching these goals closely match his or her abilities and talents.

3. *Goals That Identify Actions That Need to Be Taken:* Do your son's or daughter's educational and career goals help your teen to see those things that he or she needs to do to successfully reach his or her career dreams?

   0 *No*
   My teen's goals do not help him or her to identify and act on those things that need to be done to successfully reach his or her career dreams.

   1 *Somewhat*
   My teen's goals somewhat help him or her to identify and act on those things that need to be done to successfully reach his or her career dreams.

   2 *Yes*
   My teen's goals definitely help him or her to identify and act on those things that need to be done to successfully reach his or her career dreams.

4. *Career Exploration:* Has your son or daughter participated in any career exploration activities that really made him or her stop and think about what educational and career options he or she might want to pursue?

   0 *No*
   My teen has not yet participated in any such activities.

   1 *Somewhat*
   My teen has participated in some career exploration activities, but these activities have only been somewhat influential in getting my teen to seriously consider any future options.

   2 *Yes*
   My teen has participated in career exploration activities that were very influential in getting my teen to seriously consider future options.

5. *Meaningful and Valued Career Direction:* Has your son or daughter made any progress in identifying a career direction that he or she sees as being personally meaningful and valuable?

   0 *No*
   My teen has not yet made any progress in identifying a personally meaningful and valued career direction.

   1 *Somewhat*
   My teen has made some progress in identifying a personally meaningful and valued career direction.

   2 *Yes*
   My teen has made a great deal of progress in identifying a personally meaningful and valued career direction.

6. *Self-Defined Choices:* Is your son or daughter beginning to talk about career options that he or she is defining and preparing to pursue?

   0 *No*
   My teen has not yet begun to talk about career options that he or she has defined.

   1 *Somewhat*
   My teen is somewhat beginning to talk about career options that he or she has defined and is preparing to pursue.

   2 *Yes*
   My teen is really beginning to talk about career options that he or she has defined and is actively preparing to pursue.

Creating Effective Goals = ___ + ___ + ___ + ___ + ___ + ___ = _____ ***Total Score***

Question 1 2 3 4 5 6

Knowing Yourself

1. *Abilities, Talents, and Skills:* Has your son or daughter seriously explored his or her abilities, talents, and skills, as well as the kinds of careers that would be more likely to let him or her use these aptitudes?

   0 *No*
   My teen has not seriously explored her or his abilities, talents, and skills or the kinds of careers that would let her or him use these aptitudes.

   1 *Somewhat*
   My teen has begun to explore her or his abilities, talents, and skills, as well as the kinds of careers that would let him or her use these aptitudes.

   2 *Yes*
   My teen has a good understanding of her or his abilities, talents, and skills, as well as the kinds of careers that would let her or him use these aptitudes.

2. *Work Values:* Has your son or daughter seriously explored what work values are important and the kinds of careers that would be more likely to let your teen express these values?

   0 *No*
   My teen has not seriously explored his or her work values or the kinds of careers that would let my teen express these values.

   1 *Somewhat*
   My teen has begun to explore his or her work values, as well as the kinds of careers that would let him or her express these work values.

   2 *Yes*
   My teen has a good understanding of what work values are important, as well as the kinds of careers that would let him or her express these work values.

3. *Personality Traits:* Has your son or daughter seriously explored aspects of his or her personality that your teen would like to be able to express in a future career, as well as the kinds of careers that would support use of these characteristics?

   0 *No*
   My teen has not seriously explored aspects of his or her personality that my teen would like to be able to express in a future career or the kinds of careers that would support use of these characteristics.

   1 *Somewhat*
   My teen has begun to explore aspects of his or her personality that my teen would like to be able to express in a future career, as well as the kinds of careers that would be more likely to support use of these characteristics.

   2 *Yes*
   My teen has a good understanding of the aspects of his or her personality that my teen would like to be able to express in a future career, as well as the kinds of careers that would be more likely to support use of these characteristics.

4. *Interests:* Has your daughter or son seriously explored what interests she or he would like to pursue in a future career, as well as the kinds of careers that would support expressing these interests?

   0 *No*
   My teen has not seriously explored the interests she or he would like to pursue in a future career or the kinds of careers that would be more likely to support using these interests.

   1 *Somewhat*
   My teen has begun to explore the interests she or he would like to pursue in a future career, as well as the kinds of careers that would be more likely to support using these interests.

   2 *Yes*
   My teen has a good understanding of the interests she or he would like to pursue in a future career, as well as the kinds of careers that would be more likely to support using these interests.

5. *Working Conditions:* Has your son or daughter seriously explored the kinds of working conditions he or she would prefer (like working outdoors or indoors, pressures and stresses of the job, or the length of the training required), as well as the kinds of careers that would be more likely to have these work conditions?

   0 *No*
   My teen has not seriously explored working conditions he or she would want to have in a future career or the kinds of careers that would be more likely to have these work conditions.

   1 *Somewhat*
   My teen has begun to explore working conditions he or she would want to have in a future career, as well as the kinds of careers that would be more likely to have these work conditions.

   2 *Yes*
   My teen has a good understanding of the kinds of working conditions he or she would prefer to have in a future career, as well as the kinds of careers that would be more likely to have these work conditions.

6. *Match Between Self and the World of Work:* Has your son or daughter found an educational and career direction that has the potential to create an optimal match between his or her abilities, values, personality traits, and interests and work environments that would encourage expression of these abilities, values, personality traits, and interests?

   0 *No*
   My teen has not found a direction that has the potential to create an optimal match between who he or she is and the requirements of different work environments.

   1 *Somewhat*
   My teen has begun to identify a direction that has the potential to create an optimal match between who he or she is and the requirements of different work environments.

   2 *Yes*
   My teen has clearly identified a direction that has the potential to create an optimal match between who he or she is and the requirements of different work environments.

Knowing Yourself = ___ + ___ + ___ + ___ + ___ + ___ = _____ ***Total Score***

Question	1	2	3	4	5	6

Becoming a Successful Student

1. *Needed Academic Skills:* Is your daughter or son developing the academic skills needed to successfully reach her or his educational and career goals?

   0 *No*
   My teen is not developing the academic skills needed to successfully reach her or his educational and career goals.

   1 *Somewhat*
   My teen is somewhat developing the academic skills needed to successfully reach her or his educational and career goals.

   2 *Yes*
   My teen is clearly developing the academic skills needed to successfully reach her or his educational and career goals.

2. *Language Arts Classes:* Is your son or daughter succeeding in language arts classes?

   0 *No*
   My teen is getting mostly *D*s and failing grades.

   1 *Somewhat*
   My teen is getting mostly *C*s.

   2 *Yes*
   My teen is getting mostly *B*s and *A*s.

3. *Mathematics Classes:* Is your son or daughter succeeding in mathematics classes?

   0 *No*
   My teen is getting mostly *D*s and failing grades.

   1 *Somewhat*
   My teen is getting mostly *C*s.

   2 *Yes*
   My teen is getting mostly *B*s and *A*s.

4. *Science and Technology Classes:* Is your son or daughter succeeding in science and technology classes?

   0 *No*
   My teen is getting mostly *D*s and failing grades.

   1 *Somewhat*
   My teen is getting mostly *C*s.

   2 *Yes*
   My teen is getting mostly *B*s and *A*s.

5. *Interesting Academic Direction:* Is your son or daughter developing an academic direction in school that he or she would be intrinsically interested in pursuing?

   0 *No*
   My teen is not developing a direction in school that he or she would be intrinsically interested in pursuing.

   1 *Possibly*
   My teen may be developing a direction in school that he or she would be intrinsically interested in pursuing.

   2 *Yes*
   My teen is clearly developing a direction in school that he or she is intrinsically interested in pursuing.

6. *Self-Regulated Learner:* Is your son or daughter becoming an effective self-regulated learner, actively engaged in and committed to doing school work well and taking control of his or her learning?

   0 *No*
   My teen is not becoming an effective self-regulated learner.
   1 *Somewhat*
   My teen is somewhat becoming an effective self-regulated learner.
   2 *Yes*
   My teen is becoming an effective self-regulated learner.

Becoming a Successful Student = ___ + ___ + ___ + ___ + ___ + ___ = _____ ***Total Score***
Question 1 2 3 4 5 6

Getting Along With Others

1. *Communication Skills:* Can your son or daughter effectively communicate and get along with others at school (e.g., by showing good listening skills, speaking up and assertively stating an opinion, or being sensitive to the feelings and perspectives of others)?

   0 *No*
   My teen may have some difficulties in communicating and getting along with others.
   1 *Somewhat*
   My teen usually communicates effectively and gets along well with others.
   2 *Yes*
   My teen is very skilled at communicating effectively and getting along well with others.

2. *Diversity Skills:* Can your son or daughter get along with people from very different backgrounds (such as people who are ethnically and racially different)?

   0 *No*
   My teen may have some difficulty getting along with people from different backgrounds.
   1 *Somewhat*
   My teen is likely to mostly get along well with people from different backgrounds.
   2 *Yes*
   My teen is really able to get along very well with people from different backgrounds.

3. *Responsible Work Habits:* Does your son or daughter use responsible work habits to be successful in school (such as showing initiative, following rules and regulations, being dependable, completing tasks both on one's own and under supervision)?

   0 *No*
   My teen may have some problems in consistently using responsible work habits.
   1 *Somewhat*
   My teen is somewhat consistent in using responsible work habits.
   2 *Yes*
   My teen is very consistent in using responsible work habits.

4. *Positive Personal Qualities:* Does your son or daughter use positive personal qualities to be successful in school (such as being a leader, having good self-esteem, and presenting him- or herself in a positive manner)?

   0 *No*
   My teen may have some problems in consistently using positive personal qualities.
   1 *Somewhat*
   My teen is somewhat consistent in using positive personal qualities.
   2 *Yes*
   My teen is very consistent in using positive personal qualities.

5. *Positive Personal Balance:* Does your son or daughter approach school, home, friends, and work with a positive personal balance (i.e., they are not overly troubled by feelings of fear, sadness, shyness, or anger)?

   0 *No*
   My teen has serious problems with such feelings.
   1 *Somewhat*
   My teen has some mild difficulties with such feelings.
   2 *Yes*
   My teen does not have problems with these kinds of feelings.

6. *Entrepreneurship:* Does your daughter or son know how to become an entrepreneur? Does your teen know how to start and run her or his own business?

   0 *No*
   My teen does not know how to start and run her or his own business.
   1 *Somewhat*
   My teen knows some things about starting and running her or his own business.
   2 *Yes*
   My teen knows a lot about starting and running her or his own business.

Getting Along With Others = ___ + ___ + ___ + ___ + ___ + ___ = _____ ***Total Score***
Question 1 2 3 4 5 6

Follow Your Interests

Record the ratings that you made for your son's or daughter's interest in data, ideas, people, and things work tasks (see p. 65).

	0 *(Low)*	1 *(Medium)*	2 *(High)*
Data work tasks	______	______	______
Ideas work tasks	______	______	______
People work tasks	______	______	______
Things work tasks	______	______	______

• Graphing Your Teenager's Interview Scores •

Record the Total Score for each of the seven sections of the interview that you have just scored. When you have done this, transfer each Total Score to Figure 6.1. With a ruler, draw a single line across Figure 6.1 that connects the scores together. This will create a visual aid to see those areas that are strengths for your teen and those that need to be enhanced.

	Total Score
1. Being Proactive, Resilient, and Adaptive	______
2. Having Positive Beliefs	______
3. Creating Effective Goals	______
4. Knowing Yourself	______
5. Becoming a Successful Student	______
6. Getting Along With Others	______
7. Interest in Data Work Tasks	______
8. Interest in Ideas Work Tasks	______
9. Interest in People Work Tasks	______
10. Interest in Things Work Tasks	______

Daughter or Son's Scores by Category

	Being Proactive	*Positive Beliefs*	*Creating Effective Goals*	*Knowing Yourself*	*Becoming a Successful Student*	*Getting Along With Others*	*Interest in Data*	*Interest in Ideas*	*Interest in People*	*Interest in Things*
High	12	12	12	12	12	12				
	11	11	11	11	11	11	2	2	2	2
	10	10	10	10	10	10				
	9	9	9	9	9	9				
Medium	8	8	8	8	8	8				
	7	7	7	7	7	7	1	1	1	1
	6	6	6	6	6	6				
	5	5	5	5	5	5				
Low	4	4	4	4	4	4				
	3	3	3	3	3	3	0	0	0	0
	2	2	2	2	2	2				
	1	1	1	1	1	1				

• Figure 6.1 •
Career Development Profile

• Talking With Your Teenager About This Assessment •

Now it is time to talk to your teenager about your impressions, thoughts, and feelings. You have used your vantage point as a unique observer of how your teenager handles important life situations and the Structured Career Development Interview to assess how well your teenager is using a proactive, resilient, and adaptive approach to the present and future. Please realize that there can be a great deal of measurement error in all forms of child assessment. Because of this, your interpretations should be made in a tentative and cautious manner. Interpreting results is part of the larger strategy of engaging your teenager in a productive working alliance. We don't want your teenager to lose interest now by hammering him or her with judgments and misunderstandings.

First, let's review the basic structure for creating a career-related I-message:

When	_____	(say what the career behavior or action is that you want to focus on)
I feel	_____	(identify your feelings about the consequences of these actions for your teen's career development)
Because	_____	(say what the possible consequences could be for your teen's future)

Here are some examples of career-related I-messages appropriate for talking with Gina, the first young woman described in Chapter 5 (Gina: The Opposite of Indecisive, Pessimistic, and Immature).

When you said that you wanted to become a counselor,
I felt very good
Because of the values that you want to put into your life's work.

When you said you were concerned about how much money you would make working as a counselor,
I felt good
Because I could see that you were really thinking through a lot of the important things that go into choosing a career that would be good for you.

When you told me about being elected president of your organization,
I felt very excited for you
Because you were so happy and I thought this would give you a chance to see what a great leader you could be.

Now it's time to engage your teenager in a discussion of his or her results. Complete the Parental Feedback Form and then set up a meeting to talk to your son or daughter about the results. At this meeting, show your teen the Career Development Profile and go over what you have said on the Parental Feedback Form at the end of this chapter. Remember to use all of your good listening skills. Provide a safe and very supportive environment in which your teenager can explore the meaning and implications of this information. This is about empowering your teenager to take ownership and control of his or her future. Avoid being judge or jury. Your teenagers will one day thank you for taking the time to invest your love and concern in them and their future.

• Sharing Information About Your Teenager's Results •

What do you think about the scores your son or daughter got on the Career Development Profile (see Figure 6.1)? On the Parental Feedback Form, briefly write down career-related I-messages that you would like to share with your teenager. What areas of strength do you see? What concerns do you have?

• Parental Feedback Form •

Directions. For each of the seven targets, place a check mark next to each critical part to show whether or not this is an area of strength for your teenager or an area that your teenager needs to enhance. Then, write a career-related I-message that you would like to share with your teenager about each target.

1. *Being Proactive, Resilient, and Adaptive*

	Strength	Needs Enhancement
Direction	______	______
Commitment	______	______
Preparation	______	______
Initiative	______	______
Assertiveness	______	______
Hopefulness	______	______

Career-related I-message: Construct a career-related I-message that you would like to share with your daughter or son about this target.

When ____

I feel ____

Because ____

2. *Having Positive Beliefs*

	Strength	Needs Enhancement
Self-efficacy for challenges and barriers	______	______
Self-efficacy for educational requirements and job duties	______	______
Outcome expectations	______	______
Locus attributions	______	______
Stability attributions	______	______
Control attributions	______	______

Career-related I-message: Construct a career-related I-message that you would like to share with your daughter or son about this target.

When ____

I feel ____

Because ____

3. *Creating Effective Goals*

	Strength	Needs Enhancement
Specific and clearly defined goals	______	______
Difficult and challenging goals	______	______
Goals that identify actions that need to be taken	______	______
Career exploration	______	______
Meaningful and valued career direction	______	______
Self-defined choices	______	______

Career-related I-message: Construct a career-related I-message that you would like to share with your daughter or son about this target.

When ____
I feel ____
Because ____

4. *Knowing Yourself*

	Strength	Needs Enhancement
Abilities, talents, and skills	______	______
Work values	______	______
Personality traits	______	______
Interests	______	______
Working conditions	______	______
Match between self and the world of work	______	______

Career-related I-message: Construct a career-related I-message that you would like to share with your daughter or son about this target.

When ____
I feel ____
Because ____

5. *Becoming a Successful Student*

	Strength	Needs Enhancement
Needed academic skills	______	______
Language arts	______	______
Mathematics	______	______
Science and technology	______	______
Interesting academic direction	______	______
Self-regulated learner	______	______

Career-related I-message: Construct a career-related I-message that you would like to share with your daughter or son about this target.

When ____
I feel ____
Because ____

6. *Getting Along With Others*

	Strength	Needs Enhancement
Communication skills	______	______
Diversity skills	______	______
Responsible work habits	______	______
Positive personal qualities	______	______
Positive personal balance	______	______
Entrepreneurship	______	______

Career-related I-message: Construct a career-related I-message that you would like to share with your daughter or son about this target.

When ____
I feel ____
Because ____

7. *Follow Your Interests*

	Strength	Needs Enhancement
Data work tasks	_______	_______
Ideas work tasks	_______	_______
People work tasks	_______	_______
Things work tasks	_______	_______

Career-related I-message: Construct a career-related I-message that you would like to share with your daughter or son about this target.

When ____

I feel ____

Because ____

Congratulations! Now share the information from your Parental Feedback Form and the Career Development Profile with your teenager. Remember to use all of your good listening skills and engage your teen in a meaningful discussion about educational and career futures.

• Chapter 7 •
Mutual Actions

• Know Yourself Exercises •
Construct a Family Career Genogram

Now that you and your teenager have discussed development of a proactive, resilient, and adaptive orientation to the present and future, it is time to do an exercise together that will promote your teenager's growth and understanding of this life-enhancing approach to the world of work. One very good way to help your teenager begin to explore the meaning of work in his or her life is by examining your family's history and culture (across the generations) and your child's place in the family. So much of who we are as individuals is really an expression of the hopes, dreams, and decisions made by family members who came before us. For example, both of my grandmothers immigrated as young children to the United States from Scotland. This experience (the separation from family members and working in the New England mills in the 1920s), combined with the necessity of surviving the Great Depression (in the 1930s), fundamentally influenced their view of the world and the values (and attitudes toward work and education) with which they raised my parents. To a great extent, I am living out that life design. My view of what it takes to be successful in life has been nurtured across several generations and the ways my family adapted to the great historical events and movements of the 19th and 20th centuries. How I understand myself (and the direction I am motivated to take my life in) is firmly rooted in this family and cultural history.

Developing a multigenerational career genogram will help you and your teenager better understand your family's career story. A family career genogram is a treelike drawing that maps out family members and their relationships to each other over several generations. Family genograms have been found to be very helpful in doing individual, family, and career counseling. As you construct your own family career genogram, remember this is part of the ongoing talking and listening that you are doing with your teenager. It is a great opportunity to explore the roots of your family's values and the direction (and for what purposes) your teenager wants to now steer his or her own life. Knowing where we have come from helps us to discover where we would really like to go in the future.

Telling Your Family's Career Story: Creating a Family Genogram

Fill out the family career genogram in Figure 7.1 together with your son or daughter. Genograms can get very complex, but this one is simple, easy, and fun to do. You can add other information and other key individuals who have played a significant role in your child's development. After completing the genogram, discuss with your teenager each of the five open-ended questions that have been provided for you. Remember to use your good listening skills and actively engage your teenager in an in-depth exploration of your family's history and culture. After that, you and your teenager will summarize what you have learned and commit in writing to do something of your own choosing to enhance your teenager's development of a proactive, resilient, and adaptive orientation.

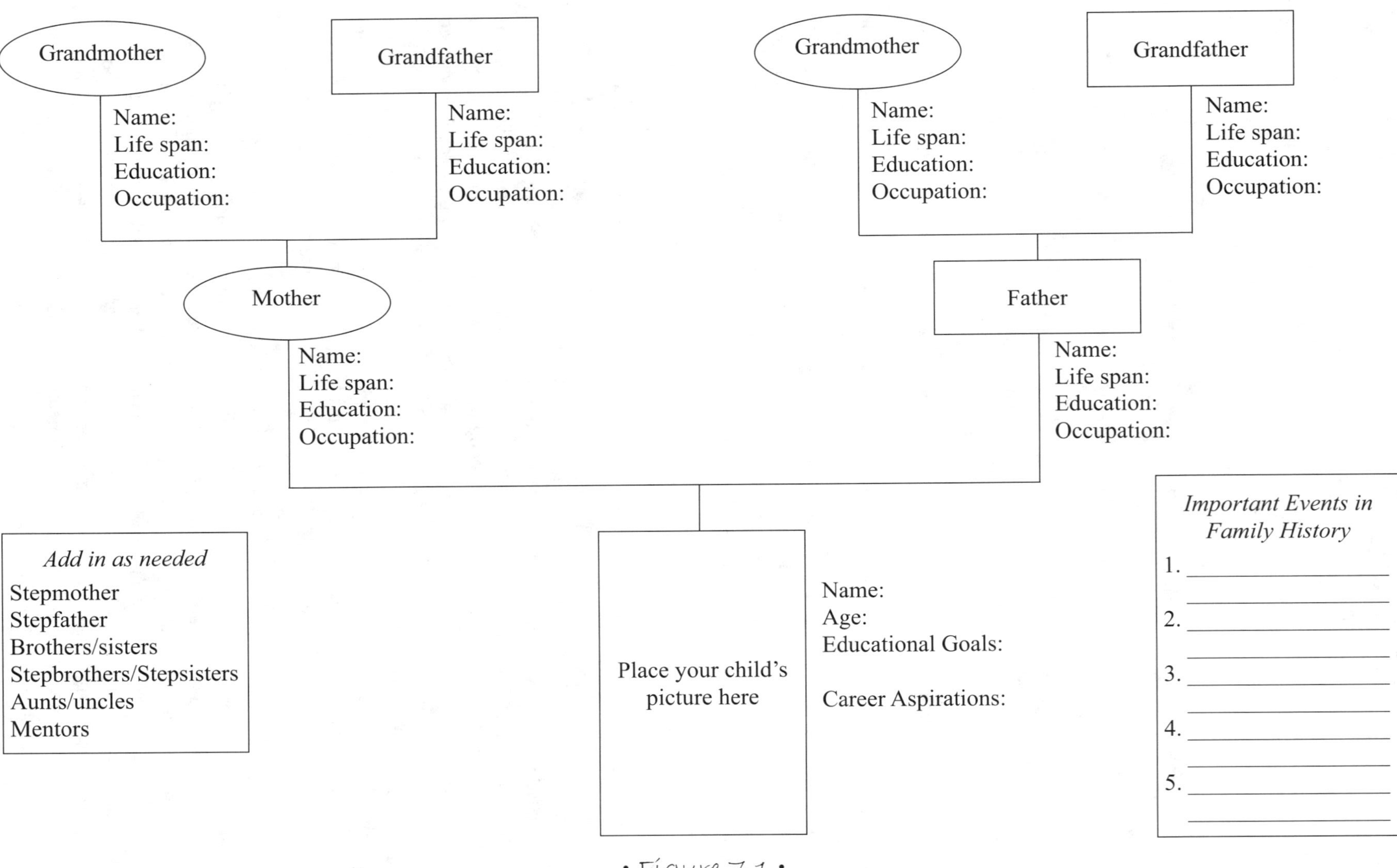

• Figure 7.1 •
A Multigenerational Career Genogram

Directions. For each family member listed on the genogram, fill in the information that is asked for (name, life span—the year born and year of death, the highest level of education each attained, and the individual's occupational title). Complete the information for yourself first. Put the year you were born. If you graduated from a 4-year college and earned your degree, put "BA" or "BS" next to education. Next, put the job title that best fits what your main occupation has been (e.g., electrician, accountant, homemaker, lawyer). With your teenager, fill in the information for the rest of your family. You and your teenager may need to explore a little and talk to other family members to gather some of this information.

As you can see, I have left the genogram tree pretty empty, listing only grandparents, parents, and your child. Of course, especially in today's world, families are way more complex than this. So add in stepparents, stepbrothers, stepsisters, and aunts and uncles as needed. Don't add too much detail, but highlight the important people who have significantly influenced how your family approaches the world of work. Who are the people who have really had an impact on your child? You might want to add a mentor that your child has had or an older brother or sister who has had a major impact on how careers are approached in your family. Include them, but leave out any uncles, aunts, or younger siblings who have not had any real impact.

Next, write down the important events in your family's history in the space provided. These might include things like immigration, the Great Depression, the *Brown vs. Board of Education* Supreme Court decision, or a divorce and remarriage. List all the critical events that have shaped your child's development.

Finally, place a photo of your child in the space provided on the career genogram.

• • •

Discuss These Questions With Your Child. Take a few minutes and discuss each of these open-ended questions with your teenager:

1. What career patterns do you see in your family?

   ____

   ____

   a. What types of fields do the men enter? ______________________
   b. What types of fields do the women enter? ____________________
   c. How does education and training fit into this picture? ____________

   ____

2. Who are the family members who have been most influential in the career choices that your son or daughter will make?

   ____

   ____

   a. What influence have they had? ______________________
   b. What family messages, instructions, or rules have been transmitted to your daughter or son about the career choices that they will make? ____________

   ____

3. What family values are expressed in the career choices people make in your family?

   ____

   ____

   a. What does this mean for your son or daughter?______________

   ____

4. In your family, how have you blended together the critical life tasks of love, work, and friendship?______________________________

   ____

   ____

5. How have important life events and historical realities influenced the career decisions made by family members and the career decisions that your son or daughter will make? These events and historical realities could include such things as the family's race, ethnic heritage, cultural background, religious orientation, economic social class, gender-role stereotypes, and immigration. Whatever is important for your family.

Summarize What You Have Learned. Next, briefly summarize what you have learned from constructing a family career genogram by answering the following questions.

Questions for Parents

1. By doing this genogram, what have you learned about your son's or daughter's career development?

2. What can you do to enhance your child's development of a proactive, resilient, and adaptive orientation to the present and future?

Questions for Your Teenager

1. By doing this genogram, what have you learned about your own career development?

2. What can you do to enhance your own development of a proactive, resilient, and adaptive orientation to the present and future?

Do a little self-reflection and then talk with your teenager about the implications of the following issues for his or her career development:

1. How has culture, gender, race, and/or ethnicity affected your career development?

2. How could culture, gender, race, and/or ethnicity affect your child's career development?

____
____
____
____

3. What can you do to help your teenager deal with the impact of factors such as culture, gender, race, and/or ethnicity on his or her career development?

____
____
____
____

• Create Your Dream Job •

To create a meaningful and personally rewarding career, your teenager needs access to accurate and up-to-date information about the world of work. Fortunately, the U.S. Department of Labor maintains a free online service that provides this information. This exercise will help you and your teenager learn how to access and use this incredible (and did I say free) resource. This exercise is designed to increase both your and your teenager's self-confidence in your knowledge of and ability to explore careers that you value and are interested in. Please follow the step-by-step instructions.

Step 1 Use an up-to-date computer that has a fast connection to the Internet. If you do not have this arrangement at home, go to your local public library. There you will find both the equipment and the people to help you. If you are not comfortable using computers, don't let this stop you! The step-by-step instructions provided here are easy to follow.

Step 2 On whatever Internet program your computer has, go to http://online.onetcenter.org/ This is the site that the U.S. Department of Labor has created for their O*NET service.

Step 3 At the top of the page you will see "Welcome to O*NET OnLine." Just below this welcome you will see three search options: Find Occupations, Skills Search, and Crosswalk Search.

Step 4 Click on Skills Search. Skills Search lets you choose from six different groups the skills that you already have or are planning to get in the future. It then matches this set of skills to all possible jobs in the U.S. economy.

Step 5 Parents go first! This is your turn to show your teenager the way. Click on the box next to each skill you would really *love* to use on a day-to-day basis when you are working. Don't worry about whether you have to go back to school or not. Don't worry about your age. Please don't let yourself be pushed around by fears that you may not be capable or smart enough to do this. Just focus on skills that would be a real dream come true if you were able to do this in the work world. Remember, it is about your dreams!

Step 6 When you have checked all the skills that might be part of your dream job, click on GO (at the bottom of the page).

Step 7 You will then see a List of Matches, occupations that match your desired skill set. Choose one that really feels to you that it would be a dream job, and click on that occupation.

Step 8 You will then see a Summary Report for that job. Briefly read the information, and Print that page.

Step 9 Under the Wages & Employment category (located at the bottom of the Summary Report page), select a state where you might want to work and click the GO button.

Step 10 Now you will see your Occupation Profile. At the bottom of the page in the box "Modify Occupational Profile Content" check all of the boxes and then click on the blue Update button.

Step 11 Briefly review the state and national wages for this job (both hourly and yearly). How much does a typical person make in this job?
Step 12 Scroll down and briefly review state and national employment trends in this occupation. Are jobs opening up or slowing down?
Step 13 Scroll down and look at the level of education required. What kind of education do people who work in this career typically have?
Step 14 Print your updated Occupation Profile.

• • •

Step 15 Now it is your son's or daughter's turn. Repeat Steps 5 through 14. Have your teenager select each skill (by clicking on the box next to each skill) that he or she would really *love* to use on a day-to-day basis when working in the future. Don't worry about whether or not your child will have the schooling necessary. Don't worry about your child's young age. Please don't let your child be pushed around by fears that he or she may not be capable or smart enough to do this. Just focus on skills that would be a real dream come true if your child were able to do this in the work world. Remember, it is about your child's dreams! Don't be judgmental.

• • •

Step 16 Now it is time to talk about this information. From the printed copies of your Occupation Profiles, look at each other's Knowledge, Skills, and Abilities and then at your Tasks and Activities. How do you and your daughter or son match up? Go back to the initial Summary Report. How do your Interests and Work Values look when they are placed side by side? What similarities and differences between you and your teenager do you see? What does your son or daughter see?
Step 17 Discuss your teenager's ideas about what an ideal job would be for him or her. Remember to use the good listening skills you have been practicing.
Step 18 Explore more! There is so much information available to you at O*NET that you need to spend time learning more about it. For example, go to your Occupation Profile and look up a related career that has been listed.
Step 19 Go to the Related Content box (at the bottom of the Occupation Profile) and find a job in your dream occupation in a state that you might want to work in (click on Most Openings). Do you see opportunities?
Step 20 Go back to the Related Content box and click on View Career Video to see a live demonstration of your dream job.

O*NET is an invaluable source of accurate, up-to-date, and free information about the world of work. The goal of this activity is to increase both your and your teenager's self-confidence in your knowledge of and ability to explore careers that you value and are interested in. The U.S. Department of Labor provides occupational information free to the public. By knowing how to use this resource, your teenagers will have a skill that they can carry across the different stages of their life. I encourage you to find the time to spend with your teenager exploring this invaluable resource.

• Examine Goals and Career Choices •

There are two parts to this exercise. First, you and your daughter or son will rate the effectiveness of Anthony's (Chapter 5, page 49) career goals. Second, you and your son or daughter will rate the effectiveness of a career goal your teenager will construct.

Anthony's Career Goals

Reread the section in Chapter 5 titled "Anthony: You Need Career Goals That Work" and discuss this with your son or daughter. Go over this example together, and get a good idea of the career goal challenges Anthony is facing. Discuss whether or not Anthony's goals meet each of the Top

10 characteristics of more effective career goals (see Box 7.1). Out of a possible score of 10, how many points did you both give Anthony? Talk with your son or daughter to make sure he or she really understands the essential parts of more effective career goals.

What was your total score for assessing how effective you think Anthony's career goals are right now? Here is how I rated them. I gave Anthony 6 out of 10. While not intended, my scoring matches Anthony's current academic underperformance in school (a C grade point average). My reasoning goes as follows. On the plus side, Anthony's career goals are intrinsically valuable to him, autonomously chosen, somewhat clear and specific, difficult but certainly attainable, closely connected to key decision-making moments, and can be realistically pursued in the social contexts in which he already lives. However, on the negative side, Anthony's career goal to become an owner of a small clothing store is not something that he consistently pursues. He does not know what actions he really needs to exert control over to become such an entrepreneur (he has some vague idea that a business degree will do it for him). And finally, he sees himself as really being on his own to bring about this personally valued future. He does not describe any support that he has received or expects to receive from others. He is on his own to secure whatever resources he needs to reach these goals.

Anthony is at risk for becoming sidetracked, going down blind alleys that lead to dead ends. If you were Anthony's parents, how would you help him reach his goals? What does your son or daughter think about this?

• Box 7.1 •

Top 10 Career Goals Questionnaire for Anthony

Yes	*No*	
_____	_____	1. Does Anthony have career goals that he really wants to go after, that he is committed to, and that he consistently pursues?
_____	_____	2. Does he intrinsically value these goals; do they mean something very important to him?
_____	_____	3. Has he chosen these goals by himself, after exploring his options?
_____	_____	4. Are his goals clear and specific?
_____	_____	5. Are Anthony's goals difficult to reach but attainable?
_____	_____	6. Are his career goals closely connected to those key moments of decision where actions need to be taken to enter a particular career path, such as doing a job search or filling out a college application?
_____	_____	7. Do Anthony's career goals show him what specific actions he needs to perform if he is to be successful?
_____	_____	8. Can these goals be realistically pursued in the regular social contexts in which Anthony lives?
_____	_____	9. Will his efforts to reach these career goals be supported by people in important social contexts such as school?
_____	_____	10. Will important resources be made available to assist Anthony to reach his career goals?
_____	_____	***Total Score*** *(1 point for every Yes answer)*

Your Teenager's Career Goals

Have your son or daughter write down in the space provided a career goal of interest to him or her right now. It doesn't have to be something your teenager is firmly committed to pursuing. You are trying to see how your child constructs effective career goals and what pieces your teenager knows how to build into these goals.

My Career Goal: ____

____

With your son or daughter, discuss whether or not his or her goal meets each of the Top 10 characteristics of more effective career goals and put the answers in Box 7.2 in the spaces provided. Out of a possible score of 10, how many points did your teenager get? Talk with your daughter or son to make sure your child really understands the essential parts of more effective career goals.

• Define Your Work Values •

This exercise will let you and your daughter or son learn about work values that are important to satisfaction in a career. Box 7.3 lists 21 work values that people often identify as being important to them (see Chapter 4 for a fuller discussion of this list). Take a moment and review these work values with your son or daughter. Talk to each other about these work values (how they have been important in your work life and how they may be important in your child's work life). This is not an exhaustive list of work values. Are there other work values that are important to you and your teenager?

• Box 7.2 •
Top 10 Career Goals Questionnaire for Your Son or Daughter

Yes	*No*	
_____	_____	1. Is this a career goal you really want to go after, are committed to, and consistently pursue?
_____	_____	2. Do you intrinsically value this goal; does it mean something very important to you?
_____	_____	3. Have you explored this goal?
_____	_____	4. Is this goal clear and specific?
_____	_____	5. Is this goal difficult to reach but attainable?
_____	_____	6. Is this career goal closely connected to those key moments of decision where actions need to be taken to enter a particular career path, such as doing a job search or filling out a college application?
_____	_____	7. Does this goal show you what specific actions you need to perform to be successful?
_____	_____	8. Can this goal be realistically pursued in the regular social contexts in which you live?
_____	_____	9. Will your efforts to reach this goal be supported by people in important social contexts, such as the school you attend?
_____	_____	10. Would important resources be made available to assist you in reaching this career goal?
_____	_____	***Total Score*** *(1 point for every Yes answer)*

• Box 7.3 •
Work Values and Preferred Working Conditions

1. Earning a high income
2. Having an opportunity to be creative
3. Helping others
4. Earning recognition or prestige in your career
5. Being able to work independently
6. Being a leader and making decisions
7. Having flexibility in your work hours
8. Having a variety of work tasks to do
9. Being curious and solving problems
10. Working indoors or outdoors
11. Using your hands and doing physical things in your work
12. Being your own boss
13. Achieving economic security
14. Working with specific tools, technologies, animals, plants, people, or ideas
15. Entering a career that requires a long training time after high school (4-year college degree or more)
16. Entering a career that requires a relatively shorter training time after high school (2-year or less associate's degree, specialized training, and/or certification program)
17. Working in an organization as part of a work team
18. Earning advancements in one's career
19. Taking risks and being adventurous either physically (such as in a special services unit in the armed forces) or in the intellectual problems or economic ventures that you pursue
20. Having the autonomy to exercise some personal control over the work tasks and problems that are the focus of your energies
21. Being compatible with your religious orientation

Parent's Top Five Work Values

Now, parents, list the five work values that are most important to you. In the space provided, briefly describe why each is so important. Talk to your son or daughter about how and why these work values have been important in your life.

Your Work Values	*Why Are They Important to You?*
1. ____________	____
	____
2. ____________	____
	____
3. ____________	____
	____
4. ____________	____
	____
5. ____________	____
	____

Your Son's or Daughter's Top Five Work Values

Now it is your son's or daughter's turn to list the five work values most important in his or her future work. In the space provided, have your teenager briefly describe why he or she feels that these will be so important. Discuss these answers together.

Your Work Values	*Why Are They Important to You?*
1. ____________	____________________________
	____________________________
2. ____________	____________________________
	____________________________
3. ____________	____________________________
	____________________________
4. ____________	____________________________
	____________________________
5. ____________	____________________________
	____________________________

Together with your son or daughter, discuss what you have learned about work values and what this may mean for your child's future educational and career decisions.

• Understand How Personality Influences Career Choices •

Box 7.4 contains a brief description of each of Holland's six personality types (for a fuller discussion of these traits, see Chapter 4). Read these together with your daughter or son. Talk to each other about your understanding of these six personality types. Have some fun, talk about some relatives or friends, and think about which personality type most closely matches them. One of the things I hope you will discover from this exercise is that most careers are comprised of a blending and shading of these six personality types. This is one of the reasons it is so important that you help your child learn more about the realities of the various work environments that he or she may one day want to pursue.

Parent's Personality Orientation

Parents go first. List the three personality orientations that best describe you in the space provided. Then briefly describe how you are or are not able to express each of these personality traits in your work. Talk to your son or daughter about how satisfaction in your job is related to these personality traits.

Holland Personality Traits	*How Are These Traits Expressed in Your Work?*
1. ________________	____________________________
	____________________________
2. ________________	____________________________
	____________________________
3. ________________	____________________________
	____________________________

• Box 7.4 •
Holland's Personality Types

Personality Type	*Description*
Realistic	These individuals like hands-on mechanical activities and tasks that are well ordered and often occur outdoors. Such people are often quite mechanically skilled and prefer working with tools, machines, and animals. They are likely to be employed in jobs such as air traffic controllers, engineers, and military officers.
Investigative	These individuals are likely to be curious about how and why things work; they are analytical and scientific. They tend not to like jobs in sales, a lot of social interaction, or work tasks that require overly repetitive activities. They are more likely to be employed in jobs such as chemists, computer systems analysts, and physicians.
Artistic	These individuals like tasks that require the creation of new forms of expression. They prefer using their imagination to grapple with ambiguous problems. These people work in areas such as creative writing, illustration, and law.
Social	These individuals enjoy working with people in helping, training, and teaching work situations. They tend not to like working with tools or their hands. They are likely to be employed in jobs such as social workers, teachers, and nurses.
Enterprising	These individuals like sales and leadership roles where they can make a profit economically and further the goals of their organization. They tend to be employed in jobs such as sales representatives, chief executive officers, and life insurance agents.
Conventional	These individuals like to perform well-ordered tasks within a clearly defined organizational hierarchy. They may prefer work tasks such as data manipulation and record keeping. They are more likely to be employed in jobs such as bank tellers, accountants, and nursing home administrators.

Your Son's or Daughter's Personality Orientation

Now it is your daughter's or son's turn to list the three personality orientations that best describe her or him. Using O*NET, identify careers that would require you to use these personality traits to be successful.

Holland Personality Traits	*Careers in Which You Can Express These Traits?*
1. ____________________	____
	____
2. ____________________	____
	____
3. ____________________	____
	____

Together with your son or daughter, discuss what you have learned about personality traits and what this may mean for your child's future educational and career decisions. If your teenager has a hard time identifying careers that express his or her preferred personality orientations, go back to O*NET and develop a list of careers that match his or her personality.

• Match Abilities, Talents, and Skills With Careers •

Box 7.5 lists the nine aptitudes included on the General Aptitude Test Battery (U.S. Department of Labor, 1979). The purpose of this exercise is to provide you and your teenager with a brief overview of some of the most commonly identified aptitudes that may play an important role in future career success. You can use these nine aptitudes to initiate a good discussion with your daughter or son. Explore how your teenager's abilities, talents, and skills will find expression in a personally valued career pathway. Do this in a way that does not limit your teenager's educational and career aspirations. As you read through this list of aptitudes, think of yourself. What abilities, talents, and skills do you use in your job?

Parent's Top Three Abilities

Parents go first. List your top three abilities. Briefly describe how you use these abilities at work. Talk to your son or daughter about how satisfaction in your job is related to using or not being able to use these abilities in your work.

Top Three Abilities	*How Do You Use These Abilities in Your Work?*
1. ______________	______________________________
	______________________________
2. ______________	______________________________
	______________________________
3. ______________	______________________________
	______________________________

Your Teenager's Top Three Abilities

Now have your son or daughter list his or her top three abilities. Then have your teenager identify careers that would require use of these abilities to be successful. Use O*NET to explore possible careers.

Top Three Abilities	*Careers Where You Can Use These Abilities?*
1. ______________	______________________________
	______________________________
2. ______________	______________________________
	______________________________
3. ______________	______________________________
	______________________________

• Box 7.5 •
Work Aptitudes From the General Aptitude Test battery

Aptitude	*Description*
General learning ability	Intelligence
Verbal ability	Understand words and the relationships between words
Numerical ability	Understand numbers and arithmetic operations
Spacial ability	Visualize geometric forms and conceptualize two- and three-dimensional objects
Form perception	See important details in objects
Clerical perception	See important details in verbal and tabular materials
Motor coordination	Adeptly coordinate eyes, hands, and finger movements
Finger dexterity	Adeptly manipulate small objects with one's fingers
Manual dexterity	Ability to move one's hands easily and skillfully

Together with your son or daughter, discuss what you have learned about abilities, talents, and skills and what this may mean for your teenager's future educational and career decisions. If your teenager has a hard time identifying careers using these abilities, go to O*NET and develop a list of careers that match your child's abilities.

• Know Your Opportunities Exercises •
A Road Map to Understand the World of Work

What you and your teenager need is a user-friendly strategy to categorize the thousands of available job titles into a coherent whole. You are in luck! The ACT World of Work Map (Figure 7.2) provides your family with a credible, research-based way to organize careers into job families based on the central work tasks involved in each career. It organizes more than 12,000 of the most common job titles into 23 job families. These job families are placed on a grid according to where each group of occupations falls on two primary work task dimensions (Data–Ideas and People–Things).

In the center of the map, you can see the two primary dimensions around which careers and job families are organized. Researchers at ACT, Inc. have long known that careers can be grouped along the People–Things and Data–Ideas work task dimensions.

People work tasks and activities include working with others to help, inform, serve, persuade, entertain, direct, and motivate them. Some People careers are teachers, salespersons, and nurses. People-related job families include education, health care, and marketing and sales.

Things work tasks include working with machines, mechanisms, materials, tools, as well as physical and biological processes. Things activities have you produce, transport, service, and repair things. Some Things careers are electricians, technicians, and engineers. Things-related job families include computer information specialties, engineering and technologies, and mechanical and electrical specialties. You can see from the map that as a career or job family has more in common with People work tasks, it is less related to Things (and vice versa). This distinction enables us to see important similarities and differences between an enormous array of job titles and work environments.

The second major dimension is Data–Ideas, the north–south axis on the map. *Data work tasks* include working with facts, records, files, and numbers. Data activities have you record, verify, transmit, and organize facts and data to get goods and services to customers. Some Data careers are purchasing agents, accountants, and air traffic controllers. Data-related job families include financial transactions, communication and records, and distributing and dispatching.

Ideas work tasks include working with abstractions, theories, knowledge, and insights and finding new ways of expressing something (e.g., through the use of words, pictures, mathematical equations, or music). Ideas activities have you create, discover, interpret, synthesize, and implement these abstractions. Some Ideas careers are scientists, musicians, and writers. Ideas-related job families include medical diagnosis and treatment, creative and performing arts, and natural sciences and technologies.

The vast majority of careers that will be available to your teenager can be ordered around this map based on the job tasks involved in that occupation. As you can see, a job family like natural science and technologies has a lot to do with both Ideas and Things work tasks but not Data and People. By using these two major dimensions, careers can be grouped together in meaningful patterns.

Think of Figure 7.2 as a giant pie that has been cut into 12 equal slices. Do you see the numbers (1 to 12) on the crust side of the slice? These slices represent how careers can be a combination of the two major work task dimensions. Each of the six career domains named in the outer crust of the pie includes two slices. For example, "Science & Technology" covers slices 8 and 9, which contain job families O, P, and Q. Research has found that each of the six career domains in the outer crust of the pie closely match Holland's six personality traits. The letter "I" just above Science & Technology means that this career domain matches Holland's *Investigative* type. The other sections also match

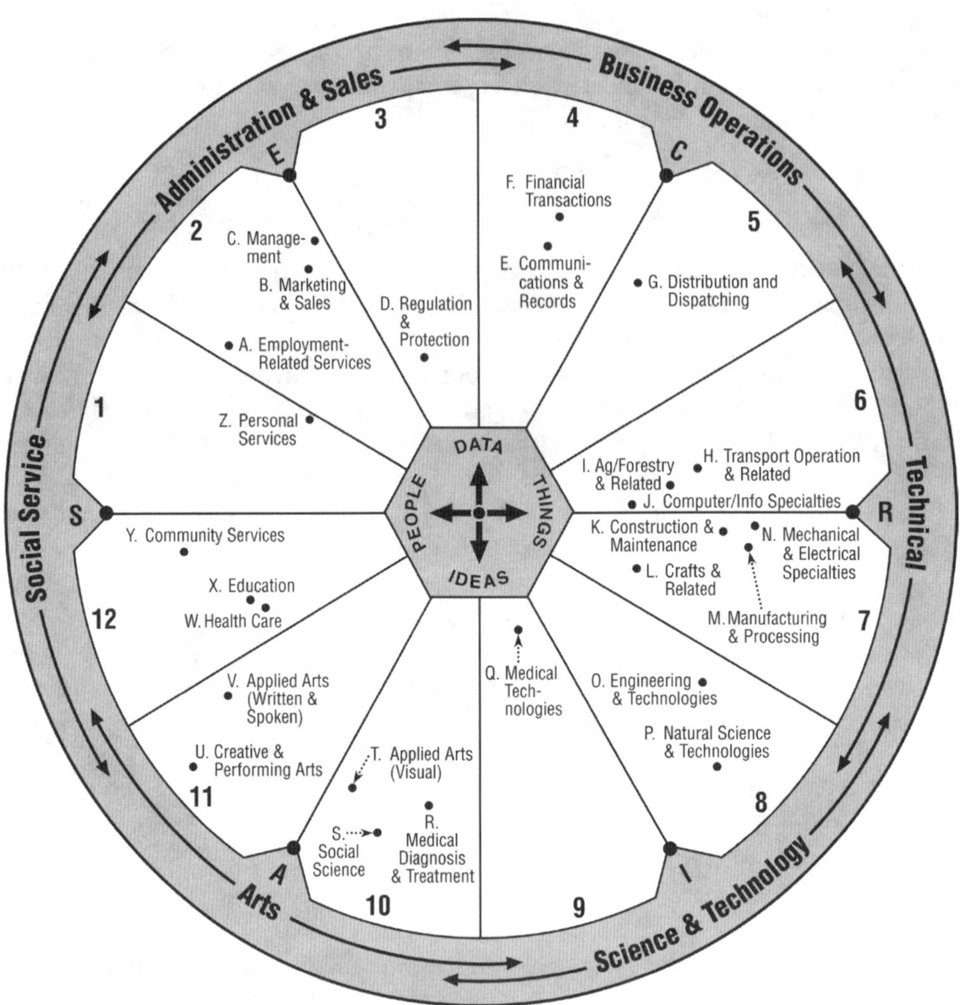

About the Map

- The World-of-Work Map arranges 26 career areas (groups of similar jobs) into 12 regions. Together, the career areas cover all U.S. jobs. Most jobs in a career area are located near the point shown. However, some may be in adjacent Map regions.
- A career area's location is based on its primary work tasks. The four primary work tasks are working with—

  DATA: Facts, numbers, files, accounts, business procedures.
  IDEAS: Insights, theories, new ways of saying or doing something—for example, with words, equations, or music.
  PEOPLE: People you help, serve, inform, care for, or sell things to.
  THINGS: Machines, tools, living things, and materials such as food, wood, or metal.
- Six general types of work ("career clusters") and related Holland types (RIASEC) are shown around the edge of the Map. The overlapping career cluster arrows indicate overlap in the occupational content of adjacent career clusters.
- Because they are more strongly oriented to People than Things, the following two career areas in the Science & Technology Cluster are located toward the left side of the Map (Region 10): Medical Diagnosis & Treatment and Social Science.

• Figure 7.2•
World of Work Map, Counselor Version, Third Edition

Note. A student version of this map is available online at www.act.org/wwm/student.html. Retrieved from www.act.org/wwm/counselor.htm. Copyright 2000 by ACT, Inc. Reprinted with permission.

Holland types: Technical matches *Realistic,* Business Operations matches *Conventional,* Administration & Sales matches *Enterprising,* Social Service matches *Social,* and Arts matches *Artistic*).

Whew, that is a lot to take in all at once. But now think of this. When your teenager takes any of the ACT achievement tests, he or she will also take (for free!) one of the best career interest inventories on the market today. The results from this interest survey will tell you what slices of the world of work your teenager is more intrinsically interested in. Information is then provided to show your teenager what careers go with which job families and what college majors lead you into these careers.

The ACT World of Work Map can be an invaluable tool to help your teenager. Unfortunately, in my experience, the results too often do not see the light of day. They will most likely stay trapped and forgotten in your child's student records. This is a real opportunity for you (provided free of charge) to help your teenager significantly increase his or her understanding of the work world in the 21st century. Take some time to become familiar with this resource.

Once again it is parents first. With your son or daughter, explore and discuss your work world and answer the following questions:

1. In what job family is your career located? ______________________________

   ____
2. What work tasks do you use in your job?______________________________

   ____
3. In what job family is the career of your spouse, partner, or a friend located?__________

   ____
4. What work tasks does your spouse, partner, or friend use in his or her job?__________

   ____

Now it is your teenager's turn to answer some similar questions:

1. Where on the World of Work Map do you think your future career will be located?______

   ____
2. Why do you think this?______________________________

   ____
3. What work tasks would you like to perform in a future career?__________________

   ____

   ____

• Around the World of Work in Less Than 26 Minutes! •

This activity will help you and your teenager learn more about the world of work. You will use the ACT World of Work Map to direct your travels. You will use O*NET to explore Job Families and careers located on the Data, Things, Ideas, and People areas of the ACT map. This process will help your daughter or son begin to find good matches in the work world that encourage expression of important parts of her or his personality, work values, interests, and work environments. Help your teenager to begin this important process of creating the best match possible. The first step is to really begin to see the wide range of choices available. Challenge your teenager to avoid becoming trapped in a corner and giving up on career pathways that could really bring satisfaction, success, and meaning to his or her work life. Take the steps described next to open up possibilities for your teenager in the world of work.

Step 1 Look again at the ACT World of Work Map (p. 94). As you move clockwise around the map, you go from Data work tasks, to Things work tasks, to Ideas, and then to People. See how the location of each job family is a match or a blending of one or two of these work task domains? Your journey with your child to learn about careers begins around this map.

Step 2 Go back to O*NET at http://online.onetcenter.org/ (save it as a favorite on your browser)

Step 3 You will again see three choices: Find Occupations, Skills Search, and Crosswalk Search. This time select Find Occupations.

Step 4 On the right, click on the arrow next to Browse by Job Family and scroll down to a job family that represents the ACT World of Work Map area for Data Work Tasks. For example, select Business and Financial Operations. Then click the GO button.

Step 5 You will see a list of individual careers that require workers to use Data Work Tasks. Click on one that strikes your interest. For example, under the Business and Financial Operations category I chose Accountant.

Step 6 You should now see the Summary Report for the Data Work Tasks job you chose. Briefly review this information and Print your Summary Report.

Step 7 At the bottom of the summary report page, choose a state that you might want to work in and click the GO button.

Step 8 You should now see the Occupation Profile. Review this information and Print a copy.

• • •

Step 9 In the box at the bottom of the page titled Modify Occupation Profile Content, select the "Wage Information, Employment Trends" and the "Education and Training" boxes. Then click the blue Update button.

Step 10 Review this information and Print a copy of the Occupation Profile.

• • •

Step 11 Now pick a job family that represents the Things Work Tasks domain. For example, I chose Architect and Engineering. Repeat Steps 4 through 10 to explore jobs in the Things domain. Remember to pick a job family that your son or daughter may be interested in.

Step 12 Now pick a job family that represents the Ideas Work Tasks domain. For example, I chose Healthcare Practitioners and Technical. Repeat Steps 4 through 10 to explore jobs in the Ideas domain.

Step 13 Now pick a job family that represents the People Work Tasks domain. For example, I chose Community and Social Services. Repeat Steps 4 through 10 to explore jobs in the People domain.

Step 14 After you have had a chance to travel around the whole World of Work Map, discuss with your daughter or son which area of the map seems to most closely match her or his values, personality, interests, education desired, and the kind of job tasks and work setting she or he prefers. Briefly record this in the space provided along with the reasons this part of the map seems to be the best match for your teenager right now. Now, choose the part of the map that is the worst match for your teenager right now and discuss why this is the case.

Best Match With the World of Work (e.g., data, things, ideas, or people)	*Reasons*
______________________________	______________________________
	______________________________
	______________________________
	______________________________

Worst Match Right Now to the World of Work	*Reasons*
______________________________	______________________________
	______________________________
	______________________________
	______________________________

• Find the Right College •

This activity will provide you and your teenager with the tools to search for the right 2- or 4-year college. With the help of the Internet and the College Board, you will be able to do this easily and with no expense. The College Board website contains an impressive array of tips and information about going to college, and this exercise will help you learn how to use this valuable resource. After completing this activity, you will be able to explore this site more completely with your son or daughter. Enjoy yourself!

Step 1 Go to http://www.collegeboard.com (click on the X in the upper right-hand corner to close pop-ups)

Step 2 You will see three choices: For Students, For Parents, and For Educators.

Step 3 Click on For Students

Step 4 Then, click on Find a College

Step 5 Then, click on College Search Engine (it is bold and underlined in the middle of the page)

Step 6 At College Matchmaker click on Start to get going. College Matchmaker will help you to identify the right colleges for your children.

Step 7 You will see eight criteria: Type of School, Location, Campus Life, Activities & Sports, Majors & Academics, Admissions, Cost & Financial Aid, and Deadlines. Select one criterion, make your decisions, and then click Next at the bottom of the page to move forward to the next one. As you make decisions about these criteria, the number of schools that match your choices will get smaller and smaller. This is the list of schools you and your daughter or son should learn more about.

Step 8 One tricky part might be the Majors & Academics section. I would suggest the following. Under Find a Major, select Browse by Category. Click on the arrow next to the Select One box. Then click the GO button. A list of majors will now pop up in the Select a Major box. Highlight each major that your son or daughter is interested in and click on the Add to List button. This will provide the information about the specific majors that your daughter or son is interested in.

Step 9 When you are making these decisions, remember what you have learned about the ACT World of Work Map and your son's or daughter's interests, values, skills, work preferences, and preferred education/training.

Step 10 When you have answered questions for all eight criteria, Print a copy of your Full Profile and save it with your other materials.

Step 11 Now spend time exploring some of the colleges that have been identified as a Good Match between what your teenager wants and what a school has to offer. Visit the websites of each of these colleges and learn for yourself what they have to offer your teenager.

Step 12 Listen to what your daughter or son has to say.

Step 13 Write down the top two or three colleges that are of interest to your son or daughter. Try to identify what needs to happen for your teenager to be accepted into these colleges.

Top College Choices	*What I Need to Do to Be Accepted at This College*
1. ____________	____________
	____________
	____________
2. ____________	____________
	____________
	____________
3. ____________	____________
	____________
	____________

• Paying for College •

Identifying the right college for your teenager is exciting, but we need to face up to what we dread the most—paying for college! You will need to spend more than 20 to 30 minutes thinking about and planning for this, but let's get started now. This exercise will help you to build your confidence and knowledge about how you are going to make this happen for your daughter or son. You and your teenager will learn about financial aid from the U.S. Department of Education, complete an estimate of what you might be expected to pay and your eligibility for federal need-based financial aid, and then search for available scholarships. In addition, you will get a chance to see the kinds of self-regulated learning strategies your son or daughter uses to take charge of important learning events. Take your time; there is a lot to learn here.

Step 1 Ask your daughter or son to organize and keep track of the financial aid information you will be learning about.

Step 2 Review the costs of going to the top colleges that you identified using the College Board search engine.

Part 1: Financial Aid From the Federal Government and the FAFSA Form

Step 3 Go to http://studentaid.ed.gov/ You can learn a lot at this site.

Step 4 Click on Funding Your Education in the "Applying for Financial Aid" section and review the information contained on this page. Look at some of the resources and publications that are available. This information will start to fill in your knowledge of the kinds of financial aid that you may be eligible for from the federal government.

Step 5 Click on Tools and Resources on the left-hand side of the page. This has links to

- Apply for Federal Student Aid
- Apply for a PIN
- And many other useful forms and worksheets

Step 6 Make sure you know what a PIN is, and follow the link to learn how to apply for a PIN.

Step 7 To qualify for federal aid, you will need to fill out a FAFSA application (FAFSA stands for Free Application for Federal Student Aid). For now, just review the FAFSA page and information. Learn about it, how to apply for financial aid from the government, and what information you will need to have in order to complete the FAFSA application when it is time for you to fill one out.

Step 8 Before leaving the Federal Student Aid site, have your son or daughter review with you the information that he or she has been recording.

Part 2: Estimating Your College Costs and Eligibility for Need-Based Aid

Step 9 Go to the website for ACT, Inc. at http://www.act.org/

Step 10 Click on Education, then click on Students.

Step 11 In the "Services" section on the left-hand side of the page, click on Financial Aid Need Estimator. This is a free service that will help you to estimate what specific colleges may cost you and what you might be expected to contribute. Remember this is only an estimate and a free exercise, it is not an official finding on what kind of financial support you and your family can expect to receive.

Step 12 Fill out this information; estimate your income and tax information if you aren't sure. When you are done, click Submit at the bottom of the page.

Step 13 At the page titled Calculation Summary, review the financial information provided. If this looks satisfactory, click on Continue to go to the next step and estimate costs for attending specific colleges.

Step 14 Pick the state where one of your daughter's or son's top college choices is located, and then click List Colleges.

Step 15 Highlight the college of interest and then click Select.

Step 16 This will bring you to the Results page. Review this information. In particular, look at the data provided under the heading Remaining Need. This is ACT's estimate of the maximum amount of money you could expect to get from this specific college as need-based financial aid.

Step 17 Review possible need-based financial aid data for your teenager's other top college choices.

Step 18 Ask your teenager to review with you the information she or he wrote down as you both went through this learning event.

Step 19 Click on the Home button to go back the ACT homepage.

Part 3: Searching for Available Scholarships

Step 20 Several hundred thousand scholarships give away more than a billion dollars each year that your teenager may be eligible to compete for! Fortunately, free search engines can track these down and help you get organized so that you can go after some of this money.

Step 21 At the ACT homepage, click on Education, then click on Students.

Step 22 In the Services section on the left-hand side of the page, click on College Search, follow the instructions, and complete the College Search. At the bottom of the page, click on the Search button.

Step 23 Review the information on a college your son or daughter might be interested in. Then click on the Admissions Financial Aid box (it is located directly underneath the red "ACT" logo). It is just to the right of each college.

Step 24 Review the information on this college, and then find the Financial Aid Sources title that is located at the bottom of the page. Click on the Free Mach 25 Scholarship Search box.

Step 25 The Mach 25 Scholarship Search will assist you in identifying scholarships your teenager would be eligible to compete for. Do either the Keyword Search or the Profile Search.

Step 26 Take your time and follow the instructions. This can be a bit overwhelming; as you will see, there are lots of scholarships available. This is a free resource you can keep coming back to until you have narrowed your targeted list of scholarships that your daughter or son will apply for.

Step 27 In the space provided here, write down the names of three scholarships that are possibilities, the application dates, and keywords that will help you to remember what the funding source is looking for and what you have to do to apply for the scholarship.

Name of Scholarship	*Application Date*	*Keywords*
1. ________________	____________	____________________
2. ________________	____________	____________________
3. ________________	____________	____________________

Self-Regulated Learner

Before ending this activity, ask your teenager to review with you the information she or he has been gathering. Once you have done this, review the seven effective learning strategies that more successful learners use. Do an honest appraisal. See if your son or daughter has done the following:

1. Identified important information.
2. Summarized the main ideas in a way that let's you organize the information.
3. Connected new information to what he or she already knew and had previously learned.
4. Taken good notes that recorded main ideas and the details to support these ideas.
5. Organized information in ways that show important relationships between the different pieces of information.
6. Monitored his or her understanding by asking questions when, for example, the financial aid information you have been gathering was not fully understood.
7. Used images or mnemonic strategies to represent important pieces of information.

This exercise gives you a chance to see some of the self-regulated learning strategies that your teenager may or may not use. If you are concerned, talk to your son's or daughter's school counselor or teachers about helping your teenager develop more effective study skill strategies.

• Starting and Owning Your Own Business •

This activity will help you and your teenager begin to learn how to start and own your own business. Having the "know how" and self-confidence to be able to "make your own job" is a treasured option now being chosen more than ever by women and minority individuals. Your teenager could become a highly successful entrepreneur. Take a few minutes to begin this journey with your son or daughter. We will take advantage of the incredible resources provided free of charge by the Ewing Marion Kauffman Foundation. Promoting entrepreneurship is their thing. We will learn about the foundation and the resources they have developed for young people to learn how to become entrepreneurs. Next, you will be able to play an online game that the Kauffman Foundation has developed with Disney to teach entrepreneurial skills to young people. And finally, as no introduction to entrepreneurship would be complete without it, we will visit the Small Business Administration's homepage. Okay, go have some fun together!

Step 1 Go to the Kauffman homepage http://www.kauffman.org/

Step 2 Look over the options on the homepage; on the top left-hand side of the page select Entrepreneurship. Read the description about entrepreneurship on the next page that comes up.

Step 3 Click on Youth Entrepreneurship Awareness. Spend a few minutes getting to know the resources on this page.

Step 4 The Kauffman Foundation has created online resources just for young people. For example, the Kauffman Foundation and Disney have teamed up to create an online game to teach entrepreneurship skills to young people. It may be a little young for your teenager, but it is really very sophisticated. At the Youth Entrepreneurship Awareness page, click on Hot Shot Business (Initiative). If this is not available, follow the directions in Step 5. Both directions will take you to the game.

Step 5 Go to www.disney.go.com/hotshot/hsb.html or http://spapps.go.com/hsb4/landing/. (The program will take a few minutes to load.) Have your teenager try his or her hand at creating and running a successful business. It is a simulation that could stimulate some good conversation with your daughter or son. Talk to your teenager about the different facets of owning your own business.

Step 6 Now go to the Small Business Administration homepage at www.sba.gov. There is a world of information and resources here that you and your family can benefit from. Explore the variety of resources provided by our Small Business Administration. They are there to serve you and help you and your children realize your entrepreneurial dreams.

Step 7 For example, click on the tab at the top of the page called Local Resources. On the map of the United States in the middle of the page, click on the state where you live. You will get information about a Small Business Administration partner that is closest to where you live. Think about contacting them for additional assistance. They can really help you and your teenager.

Step 8 Then, under Special Audiences, click on Women. Here you will find valuable resources and services to help motivate and support women who want to start their own businesses.

After you have done this, sit back and discuss the possibilities with your teenager. If your son or daughter is interested in learning more about entrepreneurship, I suggest doing two things. First, contact your teen's school counselor and ask how the school can help your teenager realize his or her entrepreneurial ambitions. Second, go back to the Kauffman Foundation and explore programs they have to get teens started early to create their own businesses. The old adage "nothing ventured nothing gained" is still true. The Kauffman Foundation has helped a lot of teenagers successfully start their own business ventures, leading to summer jobs and much more. Good luck!

• Chapter 8 •
Plan for Success!

• If You Fail to Plan, Plan on Failing •

You and your family have done a lot of good work together. Now it is time to use all of these efforts to create a plan that will help your teenager be successful. Forethought is one of our most prized human abilities. It provides us with immense adaptive advantages. Creating an educational and career plan will add this ability to your *TEAM!* Signing it will commit you and your teenager to making it happen. Many forms are freely available on the Internet for you and your teenager to use in constructing an educational and career plan. For example, the Massachusetts Department of Education has a plan that you can download and use to organize high school and postsecondary educational and career plans (www.doe.mass.edu/cd/resources). Before you go online to fill out one of these plans, arrange a time to complete the following Win–Win Contract. This final activity will help you and your teenager use all of the reflective learning and knowledge that your family has accumulated as you worked your way through this book.

• Win–Win Contracts •

Win–win contracts allow both you and your teenager to get what you want and need to be successful. Agreement is reached about the direction, goals, and supports needed to reach highly prized future outcomes. Use all of your good listening skills and insights to complete this 10-step activity with your son or daughter.

Win–Win Contract

Step 1 Have your teenager write down an educational and career direction that your child feels he or she would like to follow right now.

____

____

____

Step 2 Have your teenager write down a goal that he or she could accomplish *this* year to get closer to reaching this valued direction.

____

____

____

Step 3 Identify the assets and resources your teenager has that could help him or her to reach this valued direction. Assets and resources come from a number of sources. There are personal assets and resources (like being proactive, having positive beliefs, creating effective goals, knowing yourself, becoming a successful student, getting along with others, and following your interests). Then there are assets and resources that we get from our family, at school, and with our friends. What assets and resources does your teenager have that will help him or her to reach this valued direction?

____

____

____

Step 4 What barriers might get in the way of your teenager's efforts to reach this valued direction?

____

____

____

Step 5 How can your teenager use the assets and resources available to him or her to reach this valued direction?

____

____

____

Step 6 What courses and training experiences will your teenager need to reach this valued direction?

____

____

____

Step 7 What is the first thing your teenager agrees to do to reach this goal and follow this valued direction? To help your child, what will you do?

a. Young person agrees to: ______________________________

____

b. Parent agrees to: ______________________________

____

Step 8 What is the second thing your teenager will do to reach this goal and follow this valued direction? To help your child, what will you do?

a. Young person agrees to: ______________________________

____

b. Parent agrees to: ______________________________

____

Step 9 What is the third thing your teenager will do to reach this goal and follow this valued direction? To help your child, what will you do?

a. Young person agrees to: ______________________________

____

b. Parent agrees to: ______________________________

____

Step 10 Now both of you Sign It!

By signing below, I agree to do my part to follow the 10 steps in the Win–Win Contract.

______________________________ ____________

Daughter's or Son's signature *Date*

______________________________ ____________

Parent's signature *Date*

• Conclusion •

Congratulations! By working through the ideas and activities presented in this book with your teenager, you have provided your daughter or son with an invaluable opportunity for creative self-definition. You have placed your teenager in an optimal position in which he or she can now strive in planful ways to achieve a future that will enrich his or her life with greater meaning, purpose, and satisfaction. You have mastered the communication skills you need to form a strong alliance with your teenager. You know what targets young people should aim at to more fully develop skills that promote lifelong success. You have learned from adolescents struggling to realize these vital dimensions in their own lives. You are now armed with an assessment strategy you can use to evaluate how well your own teenager is incorporating these skills into his or her life at home, in school, and when out in the community. Together, you and your child have worked through a number of activities to see how careers fit into your family and culture. You know how to conduct free Internet searches to find careers and colleges and to figure out how you are going to pay for these dreams. And finally, in this last chapter you have developed a plan of action.

Now it is time to implement this plan. For extra support, take all of this information and show it to your child's school counselor. Please tell them that Dr. Lapan said that a professional school counselor would help you help your teenager take these steps to become the kind of adult he or she hopes to one day be. We all need support to help our children achieve career futures that enhance their lives with hope, happiness, and well-being. Please let me know how it turns out. Good luck, I like your chances for success!

• References •

Achter, J. A., Lubinski, D., Benbow, C. P., & Eftekhari-Sanjani, H. (1999). Assessing vocational preferences among gifted adolescents adds incremental validity to abilities: A discriminant analysis of educational outcomes over a 10-year interval. *Journal of Educational Psychology, 91,* 777–786.

American Psychiatric Association. (2000). *Diagnostic and statistical manual of mental disorders* (4th ed., text rev.). Washington, DC: Author.

Baker, L. (1989). Metacognition, comprehension monitoring, and the adult reader. *Educational Psychology Review, 1,* 3–38.

Bandura, A. (1977). Self-efficacy: Toward a unifying theory of behavioral change. *Psychological Review, 84,* 191–215.

Bandura, A. (1997). *Self-efficacy: The exercise of control.* New York: Freeman.

Berzonsky, M. D. (1996). Identity formation and decisional strategies. *Personality and Individual Differences, 20,* 597–606.

Betsworth, D. G., Bouchard, T. J., Cooper, C. R., Grotevant, H. D., Hansen, J. C., Scarr, S., & Weinberg, R. A. (1994). Genetic and environmental influences on vocational interests assessed using adoptive and biological families and twins reared apart and together. *Journal of Vocational Behavior, 44,* 263–278.

Blustein, D. L. (2006). *The psychology of working: A new perspective for career development, counseling, and public policy.* Mahwah, NJ: Erlbaum.

Cantor, N., & Sanderson, C. A. (1999). Life task participation and well-being: The importance of taking part in daily life. In D. Kahneman, E. Diener, & N. Schwarz (Eds.), *Well-being: The foundations of hedonic psychology* (pp. 230–243). New York: Russell Sage Foundation.

Carstensen, L. L., Isaacowitz, D. M., & Charles, S. T. (1999). Taking time seriously: A theory of socioemotional selectivity. *American Psychologist, 54,* 165–181.

Civian, J., & Schley, S. (1996, April). *Pathways for women in the sciences II: Retention in mathematics and science at the college level.* Paper presented at the annual meeting of the American Educational Research Association, New York.

Dinkmeyer, D., McKay, G. D., & Dinkmeyer, D. (1997). *The parent's handbook.* Circle Pines, MN: American Guidance Services.

Erikson, E. H. (1968). *Identity: Youth and crisis.* New York: Norton.

Flum, H., & Blustein, D. L. (2000). Reinvigorating the study of vocational exploration: A framework for research. *Journal of Vocational Behavior, 56,* 380–404.

Fouad, N. A., & Hansen, J. I. C. (1987). Cross-cultural predictive accuracy of the Strong–Campbell Interest Inventory. *Measurement and Evaluation in Counseling and Development, 20,* 3–10.

Gagne, E. D., Yekovich, C. W., & Yekovich, F. R. (1993). *The cognitive psychology of school learning.* New York: HarperCollins.

Gottfredson, L. S. (1981). Circumscription and compromise: A developmental theory of occupational aspirations. *Journal of Counseling Psychology, 28,* 545–579.

Graham, S. (1991). A review of attribution theory in achievement contexts. *Educational Psychology Review, 3,* 5–39.

Gysbers, N. C., & Henderson, P. (2000). *Developing and managing your school guidance program* (3rd ed.). Alexandria, VA: American Counseling Association.

Harmon, L. W., Hansen, J. I., Borgen, F. H., & Hammer, A. L. (1994). *Strong Interest Inventory: Applications and technical guide* (5th ed.). Palo Alto, CA: Consulting Psychologists Press.

Holland, J. L. (1997). *Making vocational choices: A theory of vocational personalities and work environments* (3rd ed.). Odessa, FL: Psychological Assessment Resources.

Jacobs, J. E. (1991). Influence of gender stereotypes on parent and child mathematics attitudes. *Journal of Educational Psychology, 83,* 518–527.

Jacobs, J. E., & Eccles, J. S. (1992). The impact of mothers' gender-role stereotypic beliefs on mothers' and children's ability perceptions. *Journal of Personality and Social Psychology, 63,* 932–944.

Kenny, M. E., Blustein, D. L., Haase, R., Jackson, J., & Perry, J. C. (2006). Setting the stage: Career development and the student engagement process. *Journal of Counseling Psychology, 53,* 272–279.

Knight, G. P., Cota, M. K., & Bernal, M. E. (1993). The socialization of cooperative, competitive, and individualistic preferences among Mexican American children: The mediating role of ethnic identity. *Hispanic Journal of Behavioral Sciences, 15,* 291–309.

Kourilsky, M. L., & Walstad, W. B. (2000). *The E generation: Prepared for the entrepreneurial economy?* Dubuque, IA: Kendall/Hunt.

Ladd, G. W. (1999). Peer relationships and social competence during early and middle childhood. *Annual Review of Psychology, 50,* 333–359.

Lapan, R. T. (2004). *Career development across the K–16 years: Bridging the present to satisfying and successful futures.* Alexandria, VA: American Counseling Association.

Lapan, R. T., Aoyagi, M., & Kayson, M. (2007). Helping rural adolescents make successful postsecondary transitions: A longitudinal study. *Professional School Counseling, 10,* 266–272.

Lapan, R. T., Kardash, C. M., & Turner, S. (2002). Empowering students to become self-regulated learners. *Professional School Counseling, 5,* 257–265.

Lent, R. W., Brown, S. D., & Hackett, G. (1994). Toward a unifying social cognitive theory of career and academic interest, choice, and performance. *Journal of Vocational Behavior, 45,* 79–122.

Levy, B. R., Slade, M. D., Kunkel, S. R., & Kasl, S. V. (2002). Longevity increased by positive self-perceptions of aging. *Journal of Personality and Social Psychology, 83,* 261–270.

Locke, E. A., & Latham, G. P. (1990). Work motivation and satisfaction: Light at the end of the tunnel. *Psychological Science, 1,* 240–246.

Luzzo, D. A., & Jenkins-Smith, A. (1998). Development and initial validation of the assessment of attributions for career decision-making. *Journal of Vocational Behavior, 52,* 224–245.

Luzzo, D. A., & Ward, B. E. (1995). The relative contributions of self-efficacy and locus of control to the prediction of vocational congruence. *Journal of Career Development, 21,* 307–317.

Mandler, J. M. (1984). *Stories, scripts, and scenes: Aspects of schema theory.* Hillsdale, NJ: Erlbaum.

Multon, K. D., Brown, S. D., & Lent, R. W. (1991). Relation of self-efficacy beliefs to academic outcomes: A meta-analytic investigation. *Journal of Counseling Psychology, 38,* 30–38.

Ormrod, M. E. (1999). *Human learning* (3rd ed.). Upper Saddle River, NJ: Merrill.

Pope, M. (2000). A brief history of career counseling in the United States. *The Career Development Quarterly, 48,* 194–211.

Robbins, S. B., & Kliewer, W. L. (2000). Advances in theory and research on subjective well-being. In S. D. Brown & R. Lent (Eds.), *Handbook of counseling psychology* (3rd ed., pp. 310–345). New York: Wiley.

Rohe, D. E., & Krause, J. (1998). Stability of interests after severe physical disability: An 11-year longitudinal study. *Journal of Vocational Behavior, 52,* 45–58.

Savickas, M. L. (1997). Career adaptability: An integrative construct for life-span, life-space theory. *The Career Development Quarterly, 45,* 247–259.

Schmitt-Rodermund, E., & Vondracek, F. W. (1999). Breadth of interests, exploration, and identity development in adolescence. *Journal of Vocational Behavior, 55,* 298–317.

School-to-Work Opportunities Act, Pub. L. No. 103-289 (1994).

Sears, P. S., & Barbie, A. H. (1977). Career and life satisfaction among Terman's gifted women. In J. C. Stanley, W. George, & C. Solano (Eds.), *The gifted and creative: Fifty year perspective* (pp. 72–106). Baltimore: Johns Hopkins University Press.

Shoffner, M. F., & Newsome, D. W. (2001). Identity development of gifted female adolescents: The influence of career development, age, and life-role salience. *Journal of Secondary Gifted Education, 14,* 201–211.

Stevenson, H. W. (1991). The development of prosocial behavior in large-scale collective societies: China and Japan. In R. A. Hinde & J. Groebel (Eds.), *Cooperation and prosocial behavior* (pp. 89–105). Cambridge, England: Cambridge University Press.

Sue, D. W., & Sue, D. (2002). *Counseling the culturally different: Theory and practice* (3rd ed.). New York: Wiley.

Turner, S. L., & Lapan, R. T. (2003a). The measurement of career interests among at-risk inner-city and middle-class suburban adolescents. *Journal of Career Assessment, 11*(3), 405–420.

Turner, S., & Lapan, R. T. (2003b). Native American adolescent career development. *Journal of Career Development, 30,* 159–172.

U.S. Department of Education. (1997). *Mathematics equals opportunity.* White Paper prepared for the U.S. Secretary of Education, Richard W. Riley. Washington, DC: Author.

U.S. Department of Labor. (1979). *Manual for the USES General Aptitude Test Battery, Section II: Occupational aptitude pattern structure.* Washington, DC: U.S. Government Printing Office.

Vondracek, F. W. (1993). Vocational identity development in adolescence. In R. K. Silbereisen & E. Todt (Eds.), *Adolescence in context: The interplay of family, school, peers, and work in adjustment* (pp. 284–303). New York: Springer.

Wanberg, C. R., & Kammeyer-Mueller, J. D. (2000). Predictors and outcomes of proactivity in the socialization process. *Journal of Applied Psychology, 85,* 373–385.

Weiner, B. (1986). *An attributional theory of motivation and emotion.* New York: Springer-Verlag.

Yinon, Y., Sharon, I., Azgad, Z., & Barshir, I. (1981). Helping behavior of urbanites, Moshavniks, and Kibbutzniks. *Journal of Social Psychology, 113,* 143–144.

Zimmerman, B. J. (2000). Attaining self-regulation: A social cognitive perspective. In M. Boekaerts, P. R. Pintrich, & M. Zeidner (Eds.), *Handbook of self-regulation* (pp. 13–39). New York: Academic Press.

• Appendix •
Effective Communication Skills

To develop good communication skills with your children, you need to become a good listener. Listening means that you do not take over a conversation. It is not about you knowing what is best or right, or about you having the most insightful ideas. Don't ruin a perfectly fine conversation by trying for a grand slam interpretation. There is plenty of time and a proper place for your interpretations. Please remember that first, last, and always, your job is to act in ways that encourage your children to continue with their exploration. Think about it; if you are the one coming up with the great ideas, doesn't that automatically take something away from your children? They are not the capable ones who can figure out solutions to the important issues that they face. Your brilliance suggests a lack in themselves and a dependency that they need to rely on you for important answers. These Top 10 Tips for Talking to Your Children were briefly presented in Chapter 3; this Appendix discusses them in more depth. The Top 10 Tips provide a balance between the skills you need to be a good listener and effective strategies you can use to get your point of view across without stopping the conversation between you and your children.

• Tip 1 •
Setting, Place, and Time

First, pay attention to the setting and conditions that will be more motivating for both you and your children to have a successful conversation. What are the optimal times when your child is open to talking? I am one of those morning people. As soon as I get up, my motor is running. However, by 2 or 3 p.m. my energy level slumps. Usually by 3:30 or 4 p.m. I rebound. So I want to get important tasks done in the morning. Unfortunately, my partner and two of my daughters don't agree with this schedule. They like to ease into their day. They pick up speed in the afternoon, so later in the day is better for them. But not when my children walk right in from school. They need time to relax and unwind. Then they are ready to talk about their day.

It is also important to identify those places and spaces where good conversations between you and your children are more likely to happen. In our kitchen, we have a little eating area (about 10 feet long). It has windows on three sides and looks out onto a yard ringed with trees. It creates the illusion of being out in the country, even though we live in town. It is a sunny and friendly breakfast nook kind of space, into which we put a small kitchen table (about 6 feet long). We fit the table in lengthwise, flush with the two middle windows. It leaves room for chairs on three sides, each with a good view of the backyard.

When my youngest daughter was a sophomore she would come home from school and immediately claim the chair at the left end of the table. She would pile all of her books in the middle of the table. (Isn't it amazing how kids carry such oversized loads in their backpacks around with them? It hurt my back just to watch her walk across the kitchen.) When she sat down at the head of the table (on the left side), she would proceed to create this comfy and secure nest around herself. Then she started right away doing her homework. (Honestly, I am not making this up. She insisted on starting her homework right away! This is definitely her Mom's handiwork. I am too embarrassed to tell you what my work style was like at 15.) My daughter would work a little and then talk a little. My wife sat at the right-hand side of the table. She read the paper, a magazine, or prepared for her tutoring lessons. My wife is a patient woman. By not pushing and rushing, she gave my daughter the control to regulate how much she wanted to say. Before long, my daughter would be telling my wife about her day (chapter and verse, in great detail). This was the time when my wife could more fully engage my daughter in a serious discussion about any issue. In successful conversations, timing is critical.

• Tip 2 •
Pay Attention to Yourself

After attending to the things around you, pay attention to yourself. The goal is to have fun and friendly conversations. So relax and have an open posture. Make sure your hands are open and inviting (no judgmental finger pointing). Body language is often much more important to the success of a conversation than what is actually being talked about. Your tone of voice is like a window into your soul. It reveals to your children your true feelings and motivations.

• Tip 3 •
Use Communication Encouragers

Smiles and up and down head nods are simple things that encourage your children to keep going in a conversation, to take some risks and not to worry if they fail. They will know that you are there to provide a safety net. When in doubt, don't say anything, just embrace the belief that your daughter or son has the capacity for self-definition, exploration, and ultimately the formation of an adultlike identity. Let this unshakable faith in your children's ultimate success get you over the little miscues and slipups that we all make in a conversation. If your relationship is solid and your motives are clear, your children will forgive these little mistakes. When you make friendly eye contact and say things like "Uh huh," "I see," and "Tell me more," it is like filling your car with high-octane fuel. Your children will have the self-confidence to look a little deeper, go a little further, and not shut down.

• Tip 4 •
Restatements

Listening is very hard work. To make the conversation hum along, you need to follow what your children are saying and where they are going. When you are not really sure, you can double-check that you are still tracking and understanding by making some very simple statements. Restatements are simple repeats and rephrases of what your child has just said. You want to keep things going but also want to be sure you are following along accurately. You can use expressions such as "So, you're saying that _____" or "It sounds like______." These expressions communicate your sincere motivation to truly understand what your child is saying. They signal to your child that you want to hear more. They empower your child to clarify any misunderstanding. And, they get you out of the way so the spotlight can continue to shine on your child's attempt to be self-reflective about his or her experiences. They keep the conversation, the exploration going. Your child doesn't end up lost in a topic and then realize he or she is alone. You need to be a team that has forged a great working alliance with each other. Simple restatements keep you connected and on track.

• Tip 5 •
Open-Ended Questions

Open-ended questions invite discussion. Why and yes/no questions close off conversation. Open-ended questions communicate your belief in your children's ability to problem solve and find meaningful patterns in their own lives. This is a real gift that you can give your children for free. But it will cost you and your children greatly if they do not discover this power that they innately have inside of themselves. I have developed a set of open-ended questions for you that you will use in the Structured Career Development Interview. They will help your children explore their thoughts and feelings about desired career futures. You will then have the opportunity to follow up with additional open-ended questions of your own.

• Tip 6 •
Reflections of Feeling and Content

Empathy may be our greatest human ability. The ability to hear, sense, and feel your child's perspective and experience of the world is a priceless gift that you bring to the conversation. Reflections of feeling and content are statements that highlight the feelings implicit in what a speaker is saying, the content, and the style or the way in which your child is saying something. For example, in Chapter 4 you met Gina (the opposite of indecision, pessimism, and immaturity). When she speaks about being elected president of her community youth service organization, her eyes light up. Her tone of voice becomes more animated. Her whole body beams in expressing the joy that this brings her. What would you say to her about this? How would you frame an empathic remark?

Empathic reflections (of feelings, content, and style of expression) create the mirror that holds out to your children a picture of who they are right now and who they might become in the future. Because of your efforts, the ideas that are being expressed by your children don't quickly disappear or get confused and entangled with other topics. You are the lighthouse by which your children can orient themselves and then proceed straightaway toward safe harbor. Reflection statements encourage your children to assume control and ownership of this process of self-exploration. Intimacy with others creates hopefulness and joy in our lives. Reflection statements communicate to your children that your role is to be a support, not judge or jury.

Use the following pattern when you want to make reflection statements. Go back to Gina for a moment. Using the format below, construct a reflection of feeling or a reflection of content statement. For example, you could say to Gina:

You feel very happy
because you are doing things you value.

Now it's your turn; write down a reflection of feeling statement that you might want to say to your child:

You feel ____
because ____

These special statements are not long, lengthy pontifications on your part. They are short and to the point. They communicate empathic understanding of what is inherently important to your children in what they have been trying to communicate to you. Say such statements tentatively. It is a good sign if your child corrects you. Listen to these corrections. They are pointing you toward what it is that they are really thinking and feeling. When you successfully use such reflection statements, you may notice your children turning toward you or looking at you more closely. Like plants orienting themselves to sunlight, we seek to be understood and find communion with those whom we love and whom we feel love us in return.

How to State Your Opinion So Your Children Will Listen

When you listen to your children, you will acquire a treasure trove of information about who they are and what they are up to. As you begin to hear what your children are really feeling, opinions and interpretations will bubble up into your awareness. At some point, you are going to want to put these thoughts and feelings into words. How can you do this without stopping the conversation? How can you give voice to your ideas without swamping and shutting down the communication exchange that you have been working so hard to make happen?

Four listening skills can help you with this: interpretation, self-disclosure, immediacy, and career-related I-messages. Each of these skills provides you with a strategy to interject your point of view without fatally rupturing the flow of communication between speakers. After gathering assessment information, you will let your children know what you think are really strengths for them or areas that could be enhanced. You can use the following skills to provide such feedback to your children without prematurely ending the conversation. Remember, it is all in how you say things.

• Tip 7 •
Interpretations

After listening to someone talk (even for a short period of time), we begin to sense themes and patterns in what the speaker is saying. The speaker implicitly suggests these ideas. They are hinted at but rarely fully expressed. It is your job, as a skilled listener, to begin to put some of these pieces together. Think of a recent conversation that you have had with a good friend. Maybe your friend was talking about something that was confusing to you. Maybe you wondered where your friend was going with the story and what was really bothering your friend about whatever the issue was. At a certain point in the conversation, you might have begun to sense that the events that your friend was talking about were not so isolated and disconnected from each other. Maybe you caught a glimpse of an idea that could act like a bridge, connecting topics that at first glance seemed far removed and cut off from each other.

Interpretations summarize these connecting ideas or themes in very succinct ways. A good interpretation will help you assist your children to gain some insight into what they are feeling. This can help your children to take control of the process as they come to better understand what these issues are. Remember always to say an interpretation in a tentative way and be willing to be wrong. If your children try to show you what they are really feeling and where your interpretation is off the mark, you are accomplishing your goal of engaging them in a process of self-exploration and intimacy. Listen to them and adjust course accordingly.

• Tip 8 •
Self-Disclosure

Your life is rich with valuable learning experiences for your children. While the world of work they will enter will be (in some very dramatic ways) markedly different from the one you know, people are people. Your experiences interacting with others and coping with the unique challenges at work posed by different life stages (establishing yourself in a position, increasing your value to your employer, earning promotions, even planning for retirement) can be of great benefit to your children. You have the knowledge to help your children place work in the broader picture of what makes for a happy, more satisfying, and meaningful life.

One way you can accomplish this is to share your own story with your children. When done properly, your self-disclosure can help your children gain insight into both themselves and the world of work they will be entering. Remember, though, self-disclosure is not an opportunity for you to go on and on as the all-knowing expert. It is not a time for you to slip in a few mini lectures!

When you feel the time is right, say your truth in a straightforward manner. Acknowledge that this was the way it was for you. It doesn't necessarily mean that it will be true in their work lives. Like any good counseling remark, a well-timed self-disclosure will stimulate and boost the conversation you and your children are having. If you notice your children's eyes looking away or the conversation seems to be closing up, back off and go right back to using your good listening skills.

• Tip 9 •
Immediacy

One of the most powerful communication strategies is to increase the intimacy of the moment between the people involved. One way to do this is to tell the person you are talking to how you are feeling about what he or she is saying and what is going on between the both of you (in the moment, in the present, right here, right now). When done properly, this can really energize a conversation and motivate your partner in very positive ways. A good way to do this is to construct a special kind of remark that helps the person with whom you are talking to be less defensive and more open to what you are saying. In the parent training literature, these have been called "I-messages." They help parents to more actively express their point of view to their children.

• Tip 10 •
Career-Related I-Messages

I-messages contain three parts. First, the parent tells the child about the specific actions the child has taken that are a cause of concern for the parent. These are events that have real consequences (either positive or negative) for the parent and child. Then the parent identifies his or her own feelings about these consequences. And finally, the parent clearly points out what the consequences of the event or actions taken by the child are. Dinkmeyer, McKay, and Dinkmeyer (1997) recommended a three-part structure (behavior, feelings, consequences) that we will use to help our work.

When _____ → I feel _____ → because _____ .

We can adapt this approach to empower you to speak to your children in ways that will create more immediacy when you are talking to them about their career development. When you are getting started, try to construct a career-related I-message that has each of these three parts (a description of the child's actions, your feelings about the possible outcomes or consequences of these actions, and the outcomes or consequences for your child). Here are two examples.

A. When you don't really take our conversation seriously about what high school courses you will sign up for next year, I feel worried because you may miss out on some great opportunities.
B. When you decided just now to take the precalculus class, I felt very good because it showed me that you weren't going to back away from a difficult challenge.

Remember, you can use career-related I-messages to emphasize things that are troubling to you as well as actions that you think are quite wonderful and exciting. Career-related I-messages help you to more effectively express your feelings and ideas to your children.